BANNERS Without Words

by jill knuth

Published by
Resource Publications, Inc.
160 E. Virginia St. #290
San Jose, CA 95112

Book Design and Illustrations: Jill Knuth
Production Editing: Scott Alkire
Mechanical Layout: Richard Kenny
Editorial Director: Kenneth Guentert
Jacket Photograph: Jennifer Knuth
Cover Mechanical: Geoff Rogers

ISBN 0-89390-075-3
Library of Congress Catalog Card Number 86-060124

Published by Resource Publications, Inc., 160 E. Virginia St. #290, San Jose, CA 95112

TABLE OF CONTENTS

DEDICATION

To the people of Bethany Lutheran Church, Menlo Park, California. For your loving tolerance when my banner designs missed the mark, and your generous expressions of enthusiasm when you were inspired by them.

1. BANNERS WOW!

Banners — they make a statement, create a mood, pose a question, present a paradox, reveal humor, and serve as an illustration or reminder. They are emphatically not just a decoration, although they can be very beautiful.

For me, banners are a way to communicate an idea visually. Deciding what to communicate in a banner is the most important part of the design process, and one that may take the most time. Even when I am making a banner for a specific occasion or illustrating a specific text, I still need to read, study, discuss, think and pray. Designing banners has turned out to be an important avenue to Bible study.

I got started in 1977. As a former art student who had spent the first years of my married life as a full-time wife and mother, I found that as my children grew older, I had more time for myself. I was asked to serve on the Worship Board at our church. Our pastor, Norm Pfotenhauer, had a strong interest in the visual arts and encouraged me to use my artistic skills. I also became interested in the evolution of liturgical worship and the liturgical calendar.

As Advent approached, I realized that this is often a forgotten season. It is the beginning of the new church year, and Pastor Pfotenhauer said that he was going to try to base his sermons on the Old Testament lessons for each Sunday. I began to see how banners could emphasize the message of each sermon, and at the same time, they could tie together the whole season of Advent.

I designed four banners, each illustrating the Old Testament lesson for one Sunday in Advent. Each could be used alone, but when they were hung together, they made a continuous picture. On the first Sunday, when the first banner was hanging alone, it didn't look like very much, and the people of the congregation later admitted that they didn't quite understand what I was trying to do. When the second banner was added to the first, the whole thing began to make sense, and people began to anticipate what would come next. By the fourth Sunday, people were really excited by the banners, and I knew that I wanted to make many more.

That was more than one hundred banners ago. As I worked, I found I had many more ideas than I could possibly make. Not every banner turned out as I had intended, and I had my share of failures. In addition to the inspiration of the lessons and sermon texts, I found that the music used in our worship was an important source for ideas. Music Director Fred Krueger challenged us with sometimes difficult, but always worthwhile cantatas and motets and anthems that were rich with visual parallels. Our present pastor, Bob Nicholus, has continued this atmosphere of cooperation and support that is so necessary for artistic expression.

When *Modern Liturgy* magazine asked readers to share things they had done in their parishes, I sent in an article about the first Advent banners I had made, which were appropriate for Cycle A in the Lectionary. The editor asked if I could also write articles with designs appropriate for Cycles B and C. I did, and became the author of a regular column on banners that ran for over three years.

Now the material from those columns has been gathered into this book. A few columns have been left out because they did not seem to fit, and I have added some new material to fill gaps and to make the chapters relate better to each other. Most of the designs, or variations of them, exist as real banners. I have sewed most of them myself, but in the past year I had the intelligent and efficient help of Karen Gill, a young art student and excellent seamstress.

All of my illustrations have been redrawn for the book. They are intended not only to serve as illustrations of the banners described in the text, but also to stand alone as line drawings. In this form, I hope that they might be useful in parishes with copy machines, as art for bulletins, Sunday School projects, etc. Limited permission to reproduce the designs, not for profit, is given on the copyright page.

My main concern in this book is with the design of banners, so I have seldom included step-by-step fabrication instructions. The details in the drawings are not necessarily intended to be followed exactly. I hope that you will use the designs as a starting point to create your own banners suitable for your parish, using the materials and skills that are available to you.

2. ADVENT

PREPARE THE WAY

Get ready, he's coming! During the season of Advent we wait for the arrival of Christ. He came to earth as a baby nearly 2000 years ago, he comes into our hearts today through the word and the spirit, and he will come again in glory at the end of time. The word *advent* is derived from the Latin word *venire* which means to come, to arrive, to come into view. Advent is the four week period when we prepare for the arrival of this special guest. We also rejoice in the knowledge that God keeps his promises, and that he will not cancel the trip.

The prophet Isaiah has written, "Someone is shouting in the desert, prepare a road for the Lord." The road should be made straight, level, and smooth. This suggests a banner that shows a road beginning from a dark, rocky place, forced through a tortuous route. Gradually, the way becomes straighter and smoother until it is upgraded to the status of a highway for our Lord.

The road, at the beginning, twists and turns, doubling back on itself, and not seeming to make much progress. The roughness of the terrain is suggested by stuffed, irregular shapes made of coarse, dark fabric in a variety of sizes. The shapes can be sewn and stuffed separately, then attached to the banner. These very dimensional elements gradually give way, in turn, to a quilted area with stitched furrows and ridges. Along the way, the road has become straighter and now has gentle curves. Finally, at the end of the journey, the road is straight, and the earth is flat and smooth.

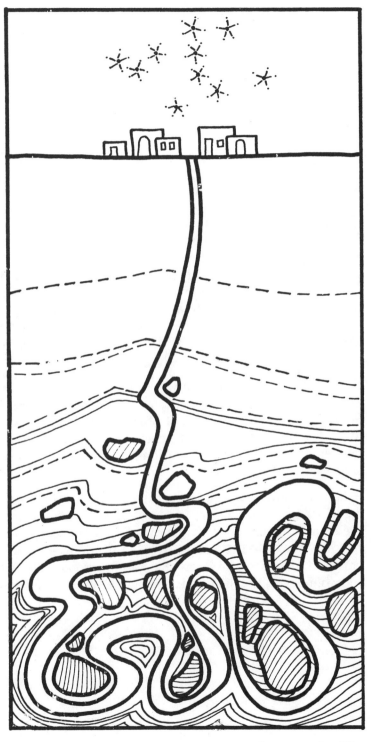

Prepare the Way

The progression of the colors and textures is important in this banner. Begin with dark browns and greys, and then change to middle value browns, greys and grey greens. Continue with slightly more intense greens, and finally, use a light clear yellow green in a smooth, soft fabric, like velour. If making a smooth color-and-value transition from greys and browns to greens is difficult, imagine that the whole road goes through a desert, and make the value transition from dark to light using only browns and greys. The suggestion of a village at the end of the road marks the arrival point and the end of the journey.

This idea of progression can be presented in an especially effective way, if the banner is made so that it moves each Sunday to reveal the next part of the road. Think of mounting the whole banner like a huge roller towel. Of course, a banner fixed in this way is stationary and cannot be used as a processional banner.

It is important that your Advent banner, as an "announcement" of Christ's coming, fits in with the other elements of the Sunday service: the readings, the music, and the spoken word. Whether designed to emphasize specific parish concerns or used at home for personal inspiration, your banner is not just a decoration; it is a visual way to present God's word.

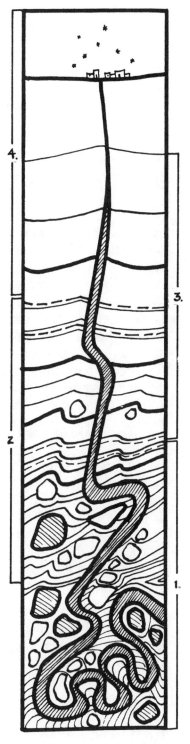

Prepare the Way

JOHN THE BAPTIST

John the Baptist identified himself as the one Isaiah had been talking about, the one who would be shouting in the desert, "Prepare a road for the Lord." Even though the title of this book is *Banners Without Words*, the use of a single word strengthens the impact of this banner. It helps us to identify the person as John the Baptist, and it focuses, in a single imperative, on the heart of John's message. In this banner, I have chosen to use the word "Change!" instead of "Repent!" because it seems to have a stronger meaning in today's English. The original Greek word is *metanoeo*, and comes from the same root as metamorphosis. If the word "Repent!" is more familiar to you, you can certainly use it.

The figure of John and his command confront the viewer immediately and directly. Secondary elements in the background are the desert, where John lived and preached, and the Jordan river, where he baptized his followers. The sun rising behind the mountain is a suggestion of the one who comes after John, who will burn the unfruitful trees and the chaff, and who will baptize with the Holy Spirit and with fire.

Use warm colors for this banner. John's robe, of course, is camel tan. Try a deep gold for the sky, and various shades of tan and brown for the desert. The Jordan river is medium blue. It will not be too prominent if the value or darkness of the blue is similar to the value of the surrounding colors. In fact all the colors of this banner will work together best if they are in the middle value range without any extreme contrasts of dark and light.

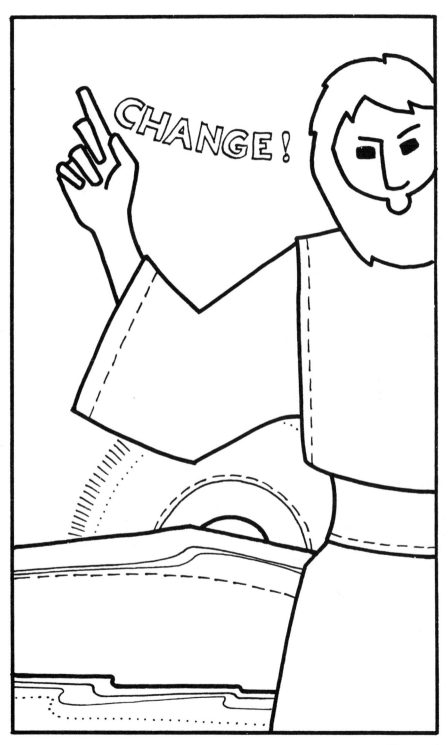

Change!

It would be fun to try fabrics of contrasting textures in this banner. Think of the rough feel of John's camel's hair robe and the sandy, rocky quality of the desert.

Use bright red-orange for the rising sun and the lettering. Layers of nylon net or tulle make an effective glow around the central disc of the sun. The cut edge of the net does not need to be finished in any way, and by increasing the number of layers of net, as you get closer to the center of the sun, you achieve a more opaque effect with stronger color.

The letters in the words are easy to make with felt. They can be securely attached to the banner with white glue or fabric glue, if you are careful to spread the glue to the very edges of the letter shapes. Sometimes I use just a few drops of glue to hold the letters in place. Then, when the glue is dry, I machine stitch around the edges of each letter. The glue seems to hold more securely than pinning or basting.

The position of the word in the design is important. Instead of being in a straight line at the bottom, like a label, it is a dynamic connection between John's head and his hand, unifying his speech and gesture into one strong admonition.

BE READY!

Be Ready! is another theme that runs through the Advent Season. No one knows the hour when the Son will appear. The example is given of the man who went away on a trip, leaving his servants in charge. Since he did not know when he would return, he told the housekeeper to keep a constant watch.

The relaxed, yet alert watchman in the doorway is silhouetted against the glow of a lamp which suggests that it is nighttime. The archway and the watchman are made out of the same dark blue, against a lighter grey background. It is important to indicate by his posture that the watchman is not asleep. He should look comfortable and at the same time wide awake. The glow of the lamp is suggested by overlapping layers of nylon net, ranging from deep yellow near the flame through light yellow, to white at the edge of the arch. The lamp base is merely hinted at by cutting away the net in the appropriate shape. Actually the lamp base and the grey background are all the same. In this way we focus attention on the glow of the light itself and avoid having to suggest any architecture or furniture in the room. It was especially fun to make the lamp flame. Instead of cutting the shape from yellow felt, I tore it, holding the felt with a pair of pliers. The fuzzy edge that resulted made a very effective flame.

Be Ready!

INCARNATION

The fourth Sunday in Advent is the Incarnation, the revelation that Jesus is both the Son of God and the Son of Man. The banner design suggests both the divine conception, and a human pregnancy, and birth. I was trying to find a middle ground between a gynecological diagram and complete abstraction.

The twelve stars that surround Mary's head are described in Revelation 12:1. Although Mary is not mentioned specifically in Revelation, this symbolism has been used to represent her in works of art throughout the centuries.

Blue is the traditional color of the Virgin and the preferred color for the season of Advent. Various shades of blue can be used effectively in this design. Try dark blue for the arch-shaped border, medium blue for the sky, and the lighter shades of blue for Mary's clothing. Use pale shades of tan, pink, peach and gold for Mary's face, the baby, the baby's halo, and the oval shape behind the baby. The dove at the top is white, and the stars can be zigzagged with silver thread, or handmade with long stitches of silver cording. I made the baby and the dove three dimensional by constructing and stuffing separate elements: a body/tail and two wings for the dove, and a body, head, two arms and two legs for the baby. Then I attached the elements onto the banner with invisible hand stitches. The effect, in the case of the baby, was almost like that of a doll. The children in the congregation found this banner especially appealing.

Incarnation

STUMP OF JESSE

Advent is a time of transition from darkness and death to new life and fulfillment in the birth of the Christ child at Christmas. Using a series of four banners, adding an additional one each Sunday in Advent, is a good way to emphasize the sense of anticipation and progression during the season. This series is based on the Old Testament readings in Cycle A of the lectionary.

These lessons from Isaiah tell about a time when people will return to God. There will be justice and peace. The stump of Jesse and the barren desert will sprout and bloom. Sorrow will give way to joy, war will be replaced by peace, and God will give his people the ultimate sign: a virgin shall conceive and bear a son.

Although each banner is independent, all four together form a unified panorama. The first banner is a mountain towering over a barren desert. This represents the mountain of the Lord spoken of in the first reading from Isaiah. The second banner continues the sweep of the desert, but in the foreground is a stump with one new branch growing out of it: the Root of Jesse from which a new shoot appears. More stems, leaves, and some buds appear in the third panel as the desert begins to rejoice and blossom. Finally a special flower opens in the last banner; the fruit of the virgin's womb.

In these banners, the background shapes of the mountain and the desert are simple, horizontal, and passive. They are made of rough, coarse fabrics in dull, dark colors. The dark stump has a heavy, broken outline in contrast to the upright, vigorous sprout. The slender, new leaves are fresh light green, and the buds are delicate pink. The brightest colors are saved for the special flower in the fourth panel, and although these colors may be strong, they should not be heavy or gaudy. A clear, bright pink works well with the lighter, more delicate pink used for the buds.

This series of banners is especially effective if the readings from Isaiah are used as the sermon texts during Advent. The banners from previous Sundays remind the congregation of the past sermons, and they begin to appreciate the connectedness and flow of the whole season.

If the construction of four banners is too big a project, the second banner, the stump of Jesse, which is mentioned in several of the lessons, can stand alone through the entire Advent season. New growth is mentioned in the selections from Romans. Paul encourages us to have hope and patience like the farmer who calmly waits for his crop to grow, and Paul gives as one of Christ's credentials his descent from David, another allusion to the tree of Jesse.

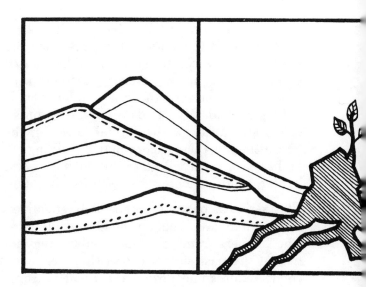

Stump of Jesse

3. CHRISTMAS/ EPIPHANY

GLORY TO GOD

The series of four banners for Advent on the preceding pages were among the first banners I created. I was very pleased with their success. Then Christmas approached, and I couldn't come up with any fresh ideas. We already had an Advent wreath, a lighted star, and two decorated Christmas trees in the chancel. Another picture of a Christmas tree, a wreath, a candle, or a star didn't seem to make much sense. It has taken me several years to realize that historically, Christmas has a very mixed past, and theologically, it's not as important as Easter and Pentecost.

In the commercial and secular world, Christmas is over after December 25, but according to the Christian calendar, Christmas day is the beginning of the Christmas season.

Historically, the various branches of the Christian church have emphasized different events connected with the birth of Jesus. The Nativity of Our Lord, celebrated on December 25, is a late-comer to the liturgical calendar. The Epiphany or the Visit of the Three Kings on January 6 is a much older festival, and formerly ranked in importance with Easter and Pentecost. It is still a major event in some parts of Christendom. For many centuries, the Baptism of Our Lord has also been connected with the Epiphany.

Glory to God

Today in the Western Church, the Christmas season begins with Christmas Eve on December 24. Christmas Day is a major festival, and the Christmas season lasts until the Epiphany of Our Lord, on January 6, another one of the six major festivals and the end of "the twelve days of Christmas." Many Protestant churches still observe Epiphany on this date, but the Roman Catholic church, in its most recent calendar revision, has moved the celebration of Epiphany to the Sunday that falls before January 6. The Baptism of Our Lord is observed on the Sunday following Epiphany, and this day marks the end of the season in which white is the proper liturgical color. In the midst of these variations in the Christian celebration of Christmas, and the conflict with secular Christmas, it is important to stop and think what the Christmas season really celebrates.

The purpose of this banner, "Glory to God," is simply to add a festive touch to a joyful day. There is no profound theological meaning behind it.

The stars are sewn like little pillows and stuffed. I used jewel-like colors of ruby red, sapphire blue, emerald green, and purple. The letters are made of a double layer of white felt, stitched around the edges for stability, and then cut out. I attached the separate elements together with hand stitching and supported them in strategic places on the back with rods of plastic plumbing pipe. An alternate way of supporting the separate elements is to attach them to a length of dark nylon net which is virtually invisible when the banner is hung.

SIGNS IN THE SKY

The Nativity of Our Lord on Christmas Eve is the fulfillment of our Advent expectations. Shortly after Jesus' birth, the angels announced the good tidings to some shepherds. At the end of Christmas, we celebrate the visit of the three kings who traveled to Bethlehem to give gifts to the baby they believed would be the king of the Jews. Their journey was guided by an extraordinary star. At the baptism of Christ, the spirit of God came down like a dove, and God's voice from heaven identified Jesus as his own dear son.

A series of banners can relate these three occasions to each other and help to unify the often neglected season of Epiphany. All three of these events are marked by supernatural signs in the heavens. God manifested his presence in the form of angels, as a special star, and in a dovelike spirit. In these banners, the divine quality of these signs is emphasized by making them abstract in shape, and transluscent in color and texture. The scale is exaggerated: most of each banner is filled with the sky and the heavenly sign, in contrast to a very small strip at the bottom that represents the earth.

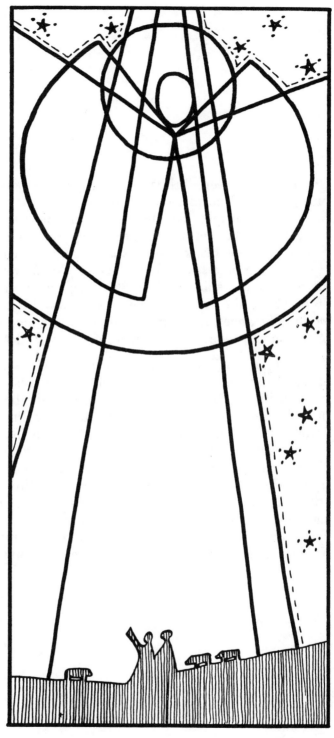

Christmas

Choose three deep, brilliant colors such as blue-purple, blue-green, red-purple, or rust-brown, for the background pieces. For contrast, use dull, flat, dark colors for the strip of earth at the bottom: for example, felt in dark blue, brown, green or black. Don't worry about the colors being realistic, like blue sky and green grass. We are representing an event and a spirit that goes far beyond the happenings of everyday life, and the colors can also be out of this world. The angel, the star and the dove are made of layers of transparent white fabric: white organdy is ideal.

Cut each layer of white, and press under ¼″ to ½″ on each edge. The shapes are simple enough so that this should not be difficult. The folded edge will not only hide the raw edge, but will also appear as a more opaque white line that will enrich the design. Pin, baste, or lightly glue the layers on top of each other, in correct position on the background. Then, stitch around each piece, going through all the layers. Consider using gold or silver metallic thread for this stitching, and if you do that, you might want to use the same metallic thread to add small stitched stars in the sky. The gold or silver adds a subtle sparkle to the banners without becoming gaudy. Apply the strip representing the earth

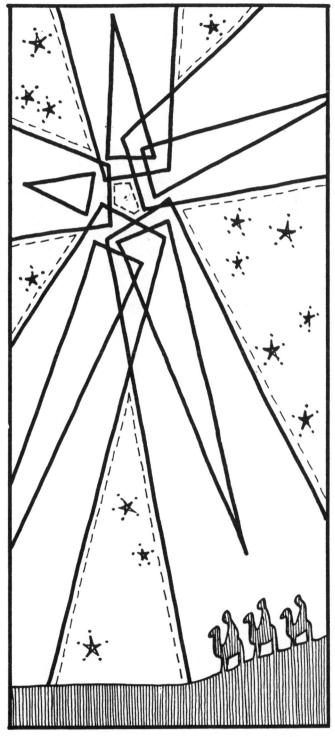

Epiphany

to the bottom of each banner. Then line each banner with a bright, contrasting color like red, turquoise, purple or golden yellow for a final festive touch.

Using related banners in a series, like these for Christmas/Epiphany, is a good way to emphasize the continuity of a season. The congregation begins to appreciate how seemingly isolated events are connected. They grow in their understanding of the liturgical calendar and the flow of the church year.

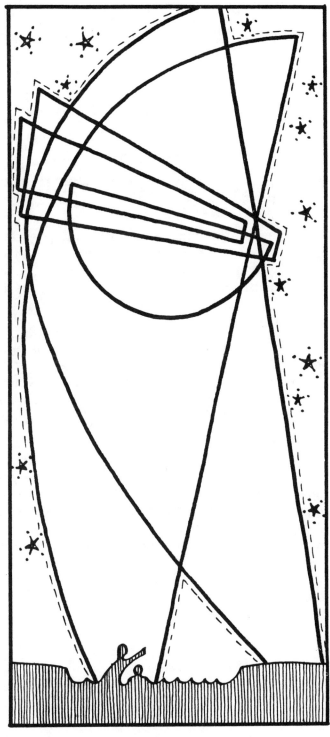

Baptism of Our Lord

SOME BANNERS WITH WORDS

We begin the Christmas season with the celebration of the birth of Jesus, and conclude it with the festival of the Epiphany, which announces the Savior's birth to the wise men from the East and, by implication, to the rest of the world. The focus for the Sunday after Epiphany is the Baptism of Christ.

In the Christmas reading in Luke 2, the angels boldly announce the birth of Christ to the shepherds. At Epiphany, Christ coming to bring light to all people is emphasized in Isaiah 9 and 60. In the account of Christ's baptism in Matthew 3, the voice from heaven reconfirms that this man is indeed God's son.

I wanted to design a series of banners that would focus on God's statements about each of these events and, at the same time, reflect the joy and excitement with which we respond to God's messages. In order to express these ideas, I worked with the quality of the lines and shapes in the designs, the way the elements are placed on the rectangular shape of each banner, and the relationships of the colors to each other. Let's look at each of these design devices separately.

He is Born

The good news of Christ's birth is announced with the sound of a trumpet. The parabolic curves in the first design go out like sound waves for the whole world to hear. In the second design, the rays from the star are pointed and aimed to pierce the darkness of ignorance and sin. The design for the baptism of Christ uses wave-shaped lines to suggest the living and spirit-filled water which John used to baptize Christ, and which cleans and nourishes us at our baptism.

The first two designs are arranged on the diagonal to give a more exciting and active feeling. In the third design, the relationship between the vertical arrangement of the hands and words and the level horizontal lines of the water show how directly and surely God pours out His grace for us. In all the designs, the elements either touch the edge of the banner or appear to extend beyond it. This supports the idea that these messages are not confined. They are intended to reach out to anyone, anywhere, anytime. They are God's pronouncements, not bound by any human limitations.

He Brings Light

I don't include words in many of the banners I design because I feel that the purpose of a banner is to communicate an idea visually, not verbally. However, sometimes a few words help to emphasize a point. Try to avoid using a lot of words. A long sentence put on the bottom of a banner is often hard to read, not very exciting, and doesn't enhance the idea much anyway. In these designs, I have not quoted directly from the Bible, but have condensed the messages to make them more direct and powerful. Keep the letter shapes as bold and simple as possible and somewhat free-form so small irregularities won't matter. There is no point in imitating letter forms that were intended to be written with a pen or printed by a printing press.

He is God's Son

In order to manipulate color successfully, it is important to remember that it has three elements, each of which can be controlled. First is the choice of the color itself, which is often the least important. Second is the element of intensity or brightness: a color of low intensity is a color that is grey or dull. The third element is value, or lightness and darkness. It is easy to confuse this with intensity. Value is easier to understand if you think of how various colors look when they are photographed with black and white film. There, everything is reduced to shades of grey ranging from black to white. When a color combination doesn't seem to work right, it is often the value relationship that needs to be changed.

Since red and green are Christmas colors, let's start with them in the first banner. Try intense red and green of about the same value for the background and the parabolic curves. Use a hot pink of a lighter value for the trumpet and the words to produce a vibrating and exciting combination. The star design suggests shades of yellow and yellow orange. Experiment with a tan or pink background and yellow-orange of about the same value for the rays. A bright yellow star and letters will stand out against this background. The water in the third banner calls for shades of blue, green and purple. Purple alternating with blue-green (both of the same value) makes a rich combination for the waves and the background. Try a lighter blue-grey or cool blue for the hands and the letters.

Since these three banners are similar in design, you might like to hang them together to emphasize the continuity of Christmas, Epiphany, and the Baptism of Christ, and to add a festive touch of color to the season.

4. LENT

SPIRITUAL GROWTH

Lent is the time when we prepare to celebrate the most important event in Christianity — the death and resurrection of Jesus Christ. In the early church, this period was used to prepare new Christians for their baptism at the Vigil of Easter. They went through a course of instruction and they also fasted.

Today we still use Lent as a time for spiritual preparation. We take stock of our spiritual state and get ready to renew the gift of baptism at the Easter Vigil. This spiritual housecleaning is represented in a banner by the image of a broom. Such an everyday implement connects Lent with the many ritual cleansings mentioned in the Bible and with the secular ritual of spring housecleaning that many people practice today, often during this pre-Easter period.

In a rural area, a good Lenten symbol is the plow which clears the fields of last year's leftover stubble and debris, and prepares the soil for a new crop.

Ash Wednesday marks the beginning of Lent. It is one of the most somber days of the year, and in many churches, the pictures and decorations are covered. Because of the austere nature of this day, it may not be appropriate to use a banner. However, if your Ash Wednesday observance permits a banner, a length of torn black fabric symbolizes (as do the ashes) the frailty and temporary quality of human life.

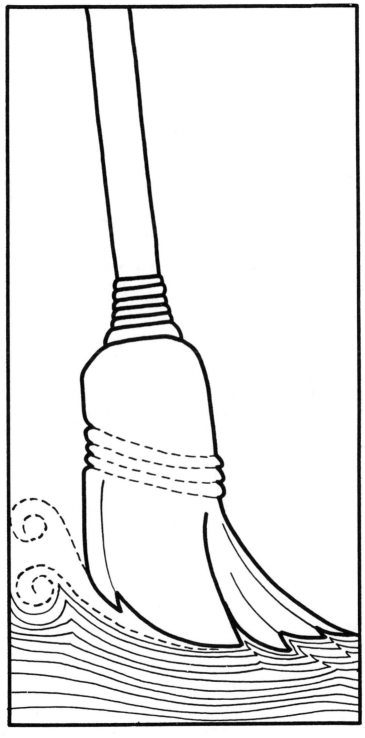

Spiritual Housecleaning

The torn black fabric is the starting point for a banner that can be used for the whole season of Lent. Since Lent is a time for reconciliation and for mending our ways, the banner is pulled together and sewn up as the season progresses. Each Sunday, another strip is stitched across the tears. Each strip bears a word representing a step in the process of spiritual healing. "Believe," "obey," "repent," "love," and "die" also relate to the readings for the five Sundays in Lent.

The account of Moses and the burning bush is the Old Testament reading for the third Sunday in Lent, Cycle C. A fire that burns, but does not consume, is a good representation for the Lenten idea of renewal out of destruction, life out of death. Moses was awe-struck and somewhat incredulous when he saw this supernatural sign. His experience reminds us that Lent is a good time to look after the spiritual part of our life even in the midst of ordinary, worldly affairs.

Each of these banners has a dark background; black, grey or dark grey-purple if you want to relate to the liturgical color for this season. The contrast between unclean and clean is heightened in the broom banner by making the left side black and the right side white. The dirt at the bottom is grey or brown. Indicate the swirls of dust with zigzagging or tacked-on lengths of cord coiled into spiral shapes. The broom is made in shades of tan with red stitching and wrapping.

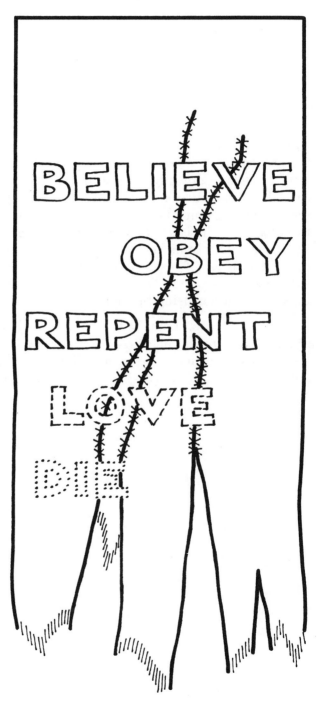

A Lenten Discipline

The flames around the burning bush are made from transparent orange and yellow fabric. Nylon organdy works well, and white organdy is easy to dye. Layers of nylon net can also be used. Don't turn under the edges of either fabric. To prevent the edges of the nylon organdy from raveling, pass the edges through a candle flame to sear and seal them. The branches of the bush and the ground are cut of one piece of black or grey, whichever contrasts best with the background. The leaves are bright green to show that they are not being burned.

Not too long ago, Lent was a dreary season of maudlin grief. These banners help to show that this six-week period is a time for reconciliation with God and our human sisters and brothers, and an occasion for spiritual growth.

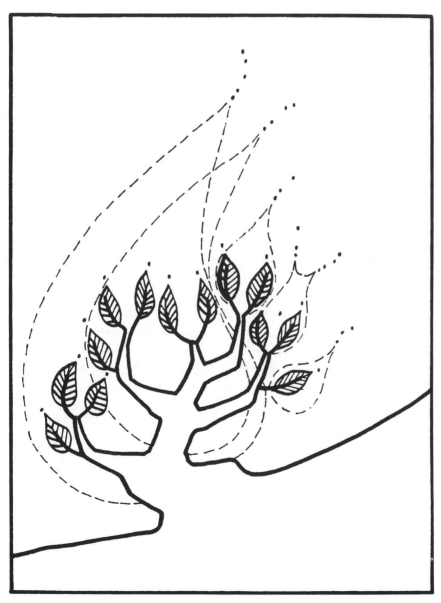

Burning Bush

SIX LENTEN CONTRASTS

Lent is a season of contrasts: sin/grace, destruction/redemption, death/life. Each of the lessons for the Sundays during this time presents a dichotomy, and each of the banners in this series is designed to show two opposite conditions: earth/heaven, dry land/living water, darkness/light, grasping/giving, death/life, and finally, the conflict between Christ's triumphal entry into Jerusalem as a hero and his death on the cross as a criminal.

Before I describe each design in more detail, let me say that making the whole series at once is an ambitious undertaking. You can choose one or two designs that underscore the Lenten emphasis in your parish for this year, then make additional banners later. The themes are general enough to be useful on many occasions throughout the year. These designs are based on the readings prescribed in the *Lutheran Book of Worship* for Cycle A. The same readings are used in the *Catholic Liturgy Book*, but in a different sequence, with the exception of the second Sunday in Lent which presents an account of the Transfiguration. The lesson about Jesus the servant, grasping/giving, is omitted from the Catholic liturgy for Lent.

Temptation

Living Water or Parched Land

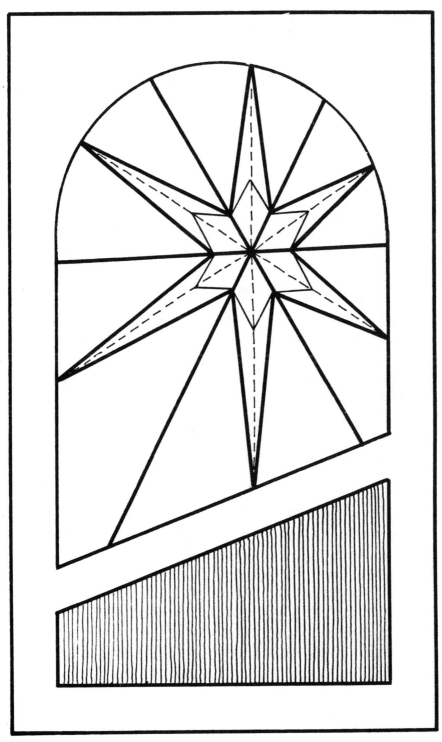

Light or Darkness

The border that surrounds each of these designs serves to separate the two situations that are depicted. I used a dull, dark purple, the liturgical color for Lent, but any dark color will create the feeling of solemnity and formality appropriate to this season. The bottom part of each banner symbolizes a situation outside of God's love and grace, while the top part suggests a Spirit-filled state. To emphasize this distinction, I used dark, dull colors in the bottom part and light, clear colors in the top part. I machine appliqued the shapes onto the banners, and used a variety of fabrics and textures.

First Sunday in Lent, The Temptation of Jesus in the Desert (Matthew 4:1-11):

This design generalizes the idea of temptation to include the apple from the Garden of Eden and the earthly forces that tend to rule our lives today: possessions, symbolized by money; power, symbolized by keys; and time, represented by a watch. The upper part of the banner reminds us to let our lives be ruled by heavenly principles.

Second Sunday in Lent, The Samaritan Woman at the Well (John 4:5-26):

The barren desert of a godless life is contrasted to the refreshing, living water that Christ offers us.

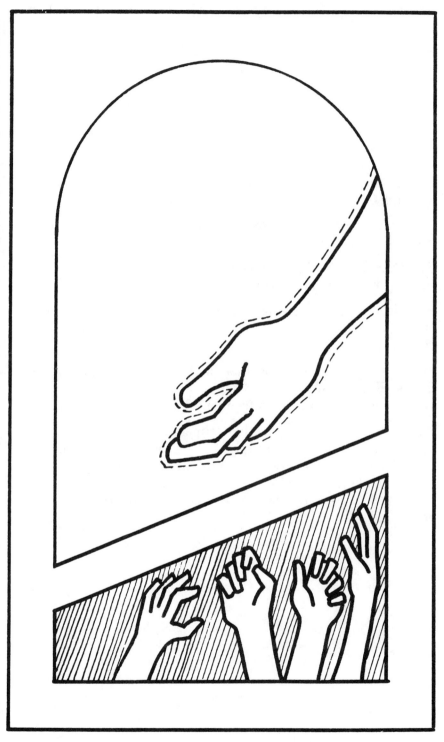

Serving or Being Served

Third Sunday in Lent, Jesus Heals the Man Born Blind (John 9:1-41):

An obvious contrast of dark nothingness compared to a glorious blaze of light.

Fourth Sunday in Lent, The Son of Man Came Not to be Served, but to Serve (Matthew 20:17-28):

A Christ-like life of serving and giving is the opposite of the helpless, selfish, grasping, and militant qualities of our human nature.

Fifth Sunday in Lent, Ezekiel in the Valley of the Dry Bones (Ezekiel 37:1-14),
and Jesus Raises Lazarus from the Dead (John 11:1-53):

The reality of physical death is superseded by life in the Spirit. Make the heart shapes in a progression of reds, going from dark on the outside to bright in the middle. This creates a glowing, throbbing effect. If you want to choose one design to serve for the whole season of Lent, this one is probably best.

Life or Death

Sixth Sunday in Lent, Sunday of the Passion (Palm Sunday), The Passion Story (Matthew 26 and 27):

The mystery of Lent is presented here as a paradox. Jesus' triumphal entry into Jerusalem, symbolized by the palms, is pictured at the bottom, while his death is represented at the top. This may seem like a somber view of Palm Sunday, but the triumphant procession takes on a broader meaning when it is seen in relation to the coming crucifixion.

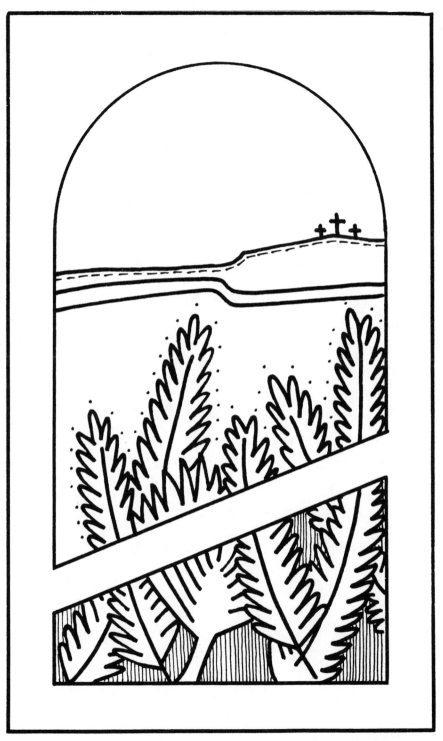

Triumph or Crucifixion

5. HOLY WEEK

PALM SUNDAY

Most of us still think of the Sunday before Easter as Palm Sunday even though the preferred name is now Passion Sunday. In the midst of the festive Palm procession commemorating Christ's triumphant entry into Jerusalem, there flows the dark undercurrent of his passion and death.

This design features the traditional palm branches and the joyful *Hosanna*. But the palm leaves point to the central portion of the banner where we see three small crosses. We are still celebrating the triumph of the King, but we begin to see that the journey leads to Calvary.

In an effort to avoid stitching around the edge of every single palm frond, I bonded two layers of green fabric together with iron-on bonding web. For variety, I used several different shades of green, including some printed fabric. From this fused material, I cut out the palm leaves. The bonding stabilized the edges so they would not fray, and, as an unexpected bonus, the strips of bonded fabric tended to curl, giving the piece a three-dimensional effect.

I attached the leaves to the banner with zigzag machine stitching, which at the same time defined the ribs and veins of the leaves.

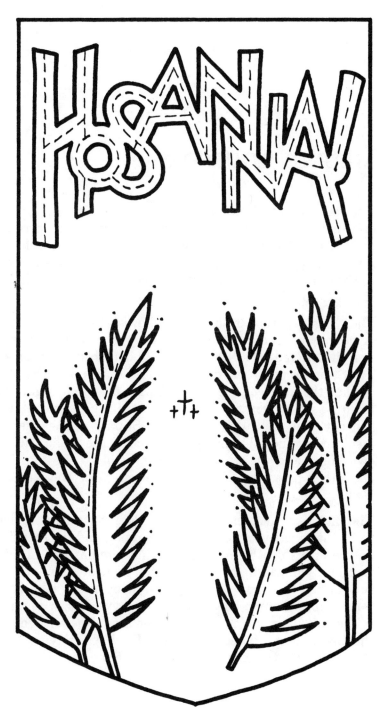

Hosanna!

MAUNDY THURSDAY

The references to Maundy Thursday from the four Gospels offer a number of ideas for banner designs. The accounts in Matthew 26, Mark 14, and Luke 22 are brief, but John goes from chapter 13 through 17 with a rich supply of themes. The central event of this day is Christ's institution of the Lord's Supper.

Many congregations re-create the Jewish Seder at this time of year. As recorded in Exodus 12, the Children of Israel were instructed to kill a young, unblemished lamb or kid. They were to paint the door posts and lintels with the blood so that the angel of death would pass over that night. The lamb was then roasted and eaten with unleavened bread. When Christ instituted the Lord's Supper at the Passover meal on Maundy Thursday, he equated the bread with his own body, and the wine with his own blood. In John 1:29 and other passages, Christ is referred to as the Lamb of God.

The historical account of the first Passover relates directly to Christ's institution of the Holy Supper, and the sacrificial nature of his death. In a banner that emphasizes this relationship, the sacrificial lamb is the central element. It is surrounded by the blood-brushed door posts and lintel. Superimposed upon the lamb is a heavy cross, a reminder of the spit upon which the Passover lamb was roasted, and the instrument of death for Our Lord. Overlaying all of these symbols is the bread and wine of the Eucharist.

Passover

Keep the color subdued; dark purple for the background, grey for the door posts and lintel, dark red for the blood, black for the cross. The lamb can be made of a fuzzy, cream-colored material and slightly padded. The lamb should be appealing yet dignified, not cute like a lamb out of a children's nursery rhyme or a Walt Disney movie. The bread and wine are the most important and prominent elements in this banner. I made the cup and plate of metallic silver cloth. The bread looks like matzo to emphasize the connection with the Passover. It is made of rough, unbleached cotton, stuffed and zigzagged with brown thread to look like a puffed-up cracker.

Foot washing is an important part of the Maundy Thursday service in some parishes. This act of humility and servanthood on the part of Christ is recorded in John 13: 1-20. The banner focuses on the rudiments of this action: a foot and some water. I felt that including a towel, hands, jug of water or other people would detract from the portrayal of this simple, humble act. The foot washing takes on a deeper meaning when we realize that Christ washed hairy, calloused, dirty, smelly feet. Depicting the foot and leg in a realistic way not only heightens the intention of this act, but avoids association with a sexy, panty-hose advertisement. Sometimes our modern-day culture gives an image quite a different connotation from what we intend.

For this banner I used a dark brown background, a terra cotta colored bowl, and flesh-toned felt for the leg and foot. The leg and toes are outlined with dark brown zigzagging, and the hair is made of large hand stitches. The water is suggested by light grey or white zigzag stitching.

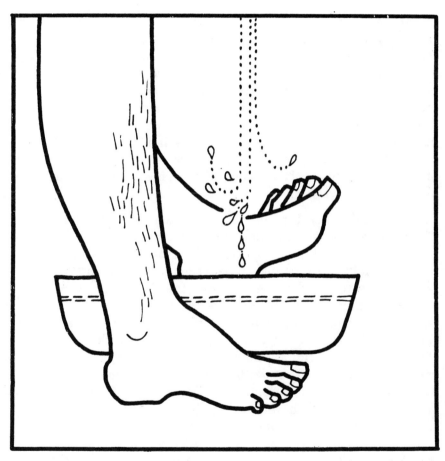

Foot Washing

In John's account of the Last Supper, he wrote down several teachings and bits of advice that Jesus gave that evening. Jesus said to his disciples, "I am the vine and you are the branches. Whoever remains in me and I in him will bear much fruit." In the third banner design, the vine and branches are presented as if they were embroided on a tablecloth. Jesus is sitting at the head of the table, and the disciples are on either side, their places indicated by their cups. The vine bears a symbolic bunch of grapes at each place. All but Judas. His branch of the vine is barren, and his cup is empty.

I used a white, linen-type fabric to represent the tablecloth. The vine pattern is machine embroidered with grey thread. I used a wide, solid, zigzag stitch. You may have trouble with the fabric tunneling under the zigzag stitch. My favorite way to avoid this is to draw the design, in mirror image, on paper from brown grocery bags. Glue two or three cut-up bags together to get a piece of paper as big as the entire design. Hand baste the paper to the back side of the tablecloth fabric, running a row of basting stitches every six or eight inches both vertically and horizontally. Then begin the zigzagging. The stiffness of the paper prevents tunneling. When you are finished with the stitching, tear away the excess paper. Not every bit of paper will come off; that is why you have worked from the wrong side which will be hidden when the "tablecloth" is sewn to the background. The cups can be made of grey satin or felt. I used a dull purple background, the liturgical color for Lent.

I am the Vine

TRIDUUM

Triduum means "three holy days" and refers to the three days that precede Easter; Maundy Thursday, Good Friday and Easter Eve or Holy Saturday. Liturgically, these three days are one continuous celebration that commemorates the central event of Christianity.

Maundy (from the "mandate" to "love one another as I have loved you") Thursday is a time for reconciliation and healing. Absolution is given for the first time since before Ash Wednesday. In the Roman rite, this is the occasion for blessing of the Chrism or holy oils, the washing of feet, and for celebrating the institution of the Eucharist. At the end of the service, the altar is stripped of linens, and the church is left in semi-darkness. No benediction is given, indicating the continuity from Thursday to Friday.

Good Friday is not a gloomy funeral but a time for meditating on the sacrifice of the Lamb of God. Liturgically, this is the simplest service of the year. There are no vestments, paraments or decorations. Instrumental music is kept to a minimum; unaccompanied singing is best. Again there is no benediction, emphasizing the unity of this three-day period.

The Vigil of Easter is the climax of the Triduum. The service begins, as the Good Friday service ended, in darkness. A light is kindled and we are reminded of creation and the resurrection of the Light of the World. The readings review salvation history, and after these lessons, new members are baptized while old members renew their baptismal vows.

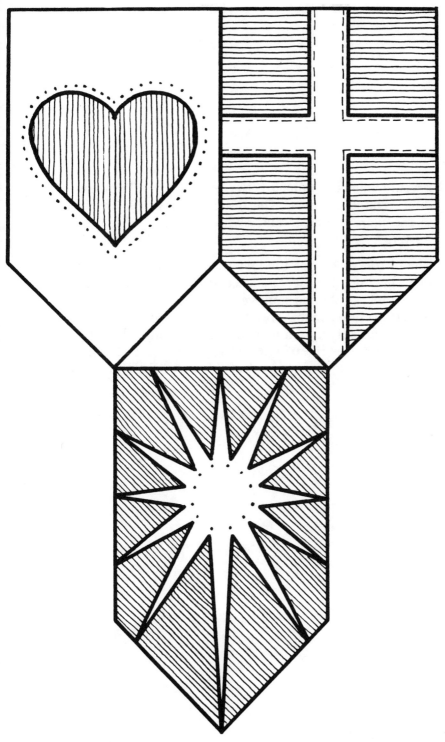

Triduum

I would like to emphasize the unity of the Triduum with three related banners. The designs are simple in contrast to the more dramatic and joyful banners you may use on Easter.

The heart symbolizes the love that underlies the reconciliation, healing, service and sacrifice of Maundy Thursday. The cross, as the most universal symbol of Christianity, is sometimes used inappropriately, but in this context, it is a strong and direct reminder of Jesus' death. The light, or sun, symbolizes the triumph of life over death; the newness of creation and the renewal of life in Christ through Baptism.

The color scheme is also simple: red, white and black. Red is the preferred liturgical color for Maundy Thursday and Good Friday, while white is used for the Easter Vigil. If the use of bold banners in a prominent position in the chancel conflicts with the solemn parts of the Triduum as it is celebrated in your parish, consider making the designs as flags or pennants. If they will be seen from both sides, it is not difficult to make them double. Or use a lightweight, semi-sheer fabric for the background, and applique the designs on both sides. Hang the pennants at the entrance to the sanctuary or overhead at the back or side of the nave. Use all three banners during the whole Triduum to emphasize the continuity of the period, but you can highlight one banner at a time by the way you hang it: higher, lower, or closer to the congregation. You can also adapt these designs as a graphic emblem to use on announcements and worship folders.

6. EASTER/ PENTECOST

LENT TO EASTER

A Tree of Death and a Tree of Life; each is a stylized cross shape. The Tree of Death has stubby, barren branches, while the Tree of Life is blooming with leaves and flowers. This pair of banners makes a good Lent-to-Easter sequence.

Even though the addition of leaves and flowers to the barren tree/cross shape expresses the idea of life out of death well enough, you can emphasize the contrast even more with colors and textures. I used a deep, rich purple for the background in the first banner. The low value contrast between the black and the purple, plus the character of the purple color itself, gave the banner a glowing, yet somber, feeling.

For the second banner, I applied the same black felt tree/cross shape to a white satin background. Although you might think that a white background would be less colorful than a purple background, the extreme value contrast (that is, the difference between light and dark) made the second combination much more snappy and lively. This effect was heightened even more by the shiny, reflective surface of the satin compared to the deep matte black felt tree.

Tree of Death

The bright flowers and leaves counteract any feeling of starkness. I used very intense, bright colored pieces of silk for the flowers and leaves. In order to minimize the work involved in finishing the edges of many little pieces, I stitched around the entire outline of each shape through a double layer of fabric. I cut each shape out, leaving about ¼" beyond the seam, then slit the middle of one layer and turned the piece right-side-out through the slit. After pressing, I had a double leaf or flower shape, with a slit on the back side. I attached the individual elements to the banner with pieces of iron-on bonding web, cut slightly smaller. The slit was thus hidden. The pieces could also have been glued or sewn on. When you are working with this many little pieces, figure out the easiest, quickest way!

Tree of Life

EASTER DAY

He is risen from the dead! This unbelievable message is the very center of the Christian faith. The Easter story, recorded in Mark 16:1-8, tells us that the women went to the tomb early Sunday morning. After not finding Jesus' body, and after receiving the message that he had been raised, they left the tomb distressed and terrified. How differently we celebrate Easter today! The psalmist anticipated the feeling we now have about the Day of Resurrection when he wrote; "Such knowledge is too wonderful for me; it is high, I cannot attain it." To this event which we are not able to understand, we respond with unbounded joy; we are "high" in today's meaning of the word.

Many visual symbols of the resurrection have been used. Since Easter coincides with spring, it is natural to associate the celebration with renewed growth and blooming flowers. A huge bouquet of fabric lilies makes a happy Easter banner. Applique the flowers to the background, or fabricate actual three-dimensional flowers with tubular stems. Calla lilies have a simple form. Use fusible interfacing to help with the shaping. The flowers should be bigger than life, and the bouquet abundant. Place the flowers in an upward, outward arrangement, with the stems hanging off the bottom, to suggest the overflowing joy we feel on this day.

Alleluia!

The butterfly is another Easter symbol. The bottom of this banner shows a dry branch and a grey cocoon. From this dead-looking environment, a brilliant butterfly has emerged. Use colors as bright as you can find. If you can buy colored silk, it works best since this fiber takes dye with more intensity than any other. Felt comes in bright colors, too, and can be assembled with iron-on bonding web (available at fabric stores), for a non-sewn banner. Try combining colors that are all of middle value, that is, not too dark or too light. If they are intense, and of about the same value, combinations like red and green, or blue-green and red-orange, set up an optical vibration. Think of a color scheme like red, purple, green and blue-green. Look at pictures of real butterflies, then design your own supernatural insect, making it bolder and more dramatic than life. Place the butterfly high on a long banner.

Death to life, darkness to light. The sun is the main source of light and life in our physical world, just as Christ is the source of light and life in the spiritual world. Imagine a radiating patchwork sun in brilliant shades of yellow against a white satin sky. Use the most intense shades of pure yellow. It is important in this design that the different shades of yellow are not too different from each other in their quality of yellow, or in the darkness of the color. For subtle variety, rely mostly on different textures, or possibly a very small flower print or dot pattern. The shape of the sun with its outward-flowing rays, expresses the glory of Easter.

Resurrection

Since Easter banners will often be used in processionals, they can be designed to move in interesting ways. Add streamers to the banner, or make the whole banner out of a free-flowing material such as light silk or polyester chiffon. Bunches of helium-filled balloons can be used as three-dimensional banners. When a banner is used as a processional banner, it is important to be sure it looks nice from the back as well as the front. Lining the banner is the easiest way to hide stitches and thread ends. Choose a bright accent color, or a small print that is compatible with the design on the front of the banner. If there is only a small amount of neatly done stitching, or if the banner has been assembled without sewing, it is not necessary to use a lining if the edges are hemmed or bound.

If you have not yet tried making banners, Easter is a good time to start. The message of life is clear, and the feeling of joy is strong. Color alone can contribute to the Easter spirit. Almost any design made with a happy heart will work. Have a glorious Easter!

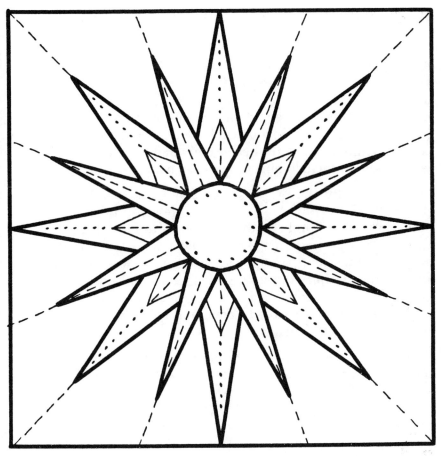

Easter Radiance

EASTER SEASON AND ASCENSION

Although we don't know what Christ actually looked like, artists since the beginning of Christianity have portrayed him. For a long time in my own work, I limited myself to designs based on nature and on symbols, and I avoided trying to represent the Son of God. But since Christ is the central figure in our faith, I eventually had to face the problem of how to include him in my designs.

The readings for the Easter season give us several different pictures of our Savior. The Gospel lessons, taken from John, tell of the appearances Jesus made to his disciples in the 40 days between his resurrection on Easter morning, and his ascension. His physical presence was real; he showed the disciples the scars on his hands and side. At the same time, he possessed a supernatural quality; he materialized through closed doors, and was sometimes unrecognizable to his friends.

The book of Revelation is the source of the second lessons for the Sundays in Easter in Cycle C. John records the vision he had of Christ as a glowing man, dressed in the purple robe of a priest and the golden girdle of a king. In one hand he held seven stars, and in the other, the keys to Hell. In his mouth was a two-edged sword which represented the Word.

The dual nature of Christ as both a human person and the divine Son of God, gives us at least two ways to portray him.

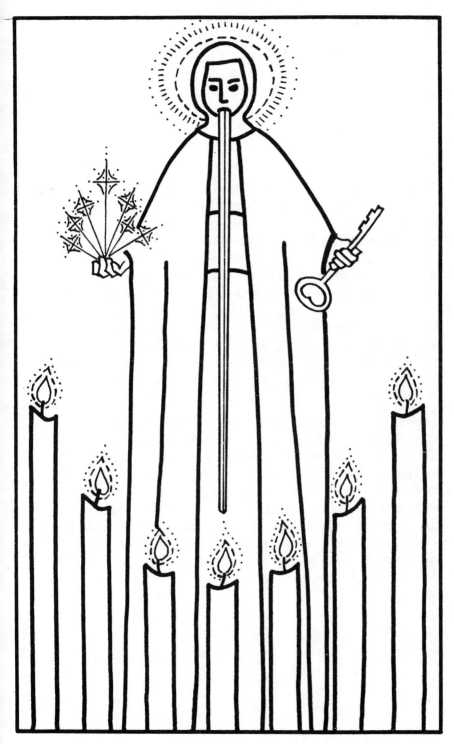

One Like the Son of Man

The first design represents the man described by John in Revelation. The figure is stylized and elongated to suggest majesty. The color and value contrasts are particularly important here. The face and hands of Christ along with the undergarment and the candles are all white. The outer robe is rich purple. Make the sword that extends from his mouth, and the seven stars in his hand of metallic silver cloth, and the wide belt and the key of metallic gold. The background can either be a very dark color, or a very bright one like bright green, bright pink, bright orange, or bright yellow-gold. Consider using layers of transparent fabric like organdy or bridal tulle to give this banner a mystical, surreal quality.

The earthly qualities of Christ are emphasized in the second design. We see him as a real man, surrounded by his friends. And yet, his attitude and their reactions show us that this is not quite an everyday occasion. Here, the figures are short and down-to-earth; they almost have a cartoon quality. I have struggled against the influence of the sentimental bible pictures I looked at in my childhood. The bible stories illustrated by the Dutch artist, Kees de Kort, are among the best today, and this banner design is done in his style.

The Risen Christ Appears

Use rich, dark colors for this banner, except for the figure of Christ, which is white. This contrast will suggest that during the time between Easter and Ascension, Christ combines human qualities with an other-worldly aspect. If you want to emphasize the spiritual feeling even more, make the Christ figure out of transparent fabric against an opaque, slightly textured background. If you can find fabrics with subtle, dark stripes, they would make good robes for the friends.

In the third design, the scarred hands giving a blessing of peace to the world, portray Christ in a symbolic way, rather than as a whole figure. I made this banner with clear, medium colors for the sky, the hills and the foreground (which can be earth or water). Transparent fabric, this time a medium brown silk organdy, worked well for the hands. The hands were outlined and the scars indicated with zig-zag stitching.

The last design depicts Christ the King in heavenly glory. This banner can be used on Ascension as well as on Transfiguration and Christ-the-King Sunday at the end of the church year.

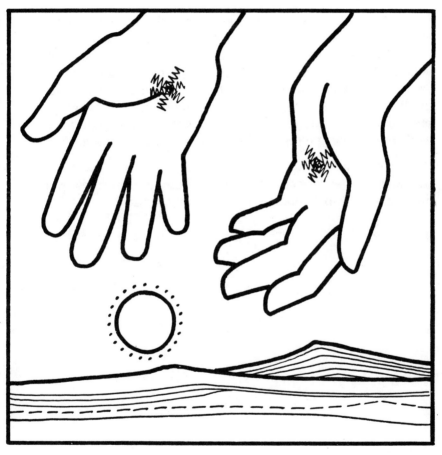

Peace I Give to You

Use rich, bright, royal colors against the foil of neutral gray clouds. Christ's robe is pure white, and the sky is a bright color like medium purple, bright pink or orange, or rich yellow. If you like to do fancy applique, patchwork or embroidery, Christ's halo can be richly embellished. Use bright, jewel-like colors, lots of contrast, and perhaps metallic gold thread or fabric. It is easier to do this detailed work before the halo is applied to the complete banner.

It is important in this design that Christ's hands extend to the edge of the banner. This emphasizes that he rules over all. His kingship is not restricted in any way.

Christ the King

PENTECOST

Have you got the Spirit? The early disciples were filled with the Holy Spirit in a very dramatic way, described in Acts 2. They were assembled on the day of the Jewish Pentecost, when a strong wind filled the house, and tongues of flame touched each person. No one understood what was happening until Peter stood up and explained how Jesus was the Son of God, and urged everyone to turn away from their sins, be baptized in the name of Jesus, and receive the Holy Spirit.

The surreal imagery used in this account suggests exciting possibilities for Pentecost banners. The spirit is described as a strong wind that filled the house. This is an appropriate image since the word "spirit" is *pneuma* in Greek, and means a breath, a wind or a breeze. Although the wind itself is invisible, we can see its effect on other things. The first banner design shows the wind coming into the house through an open window, whipping the curtains. Fresh air is blowing away the old, stale atmosphere. There is a noticeable change, a sense of anticipation and renewal.

The window frame is suggested as a simple silhouette; black felt would work well. In keeping with the liturgical color for Pentecost, and the mention of fire and blood in Acts 2, the background color behind the window is red. The curtains themselves are made like an actual pair of sheer curtains, tacked to the banner with a few stitches here and there, so that they look like they are being blown by the wind.

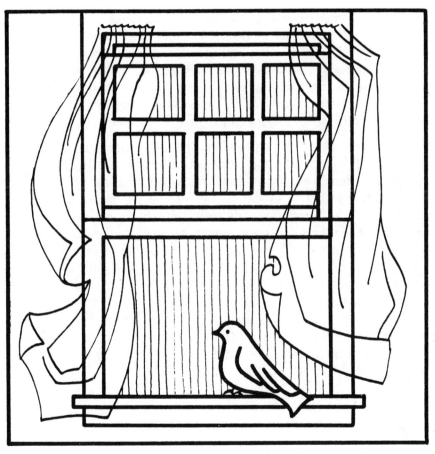

Breath of a Mighty Wind

In the Pentecost account, the Spirit is described as wind and as fire, but in other passages, notably at the baptism of Christ, the Spirit takes the familiar form of a dove. If you want to reinforce the idea of the Holy Spirit in this banner, add a dove to the composition. It can be a white dove sitting boldly on the window sill, or a dove merely suggested by a stitched outline, flying through the window.

We are given the power of the Holy Spirit in order to share it with others. This works the same way a single candle flame can be divided over and over without diminishing its own light. A receding row of candles gives the feeling that the presence of the Spirit extends infinitely through time and space. This is another opportunity to use shades of red, orange and pink. If red candles look too much like Christmas, try orange candles on a red, rust, or pink background. If you have access to many shades of red and orange, and a lot of patience, you can achieve a very dramatic effect by controlling the color and value of each candle. Start with dark, dull colors for both the candle and the background on the left, and progress in gradual steps to light, bright colors on the right.

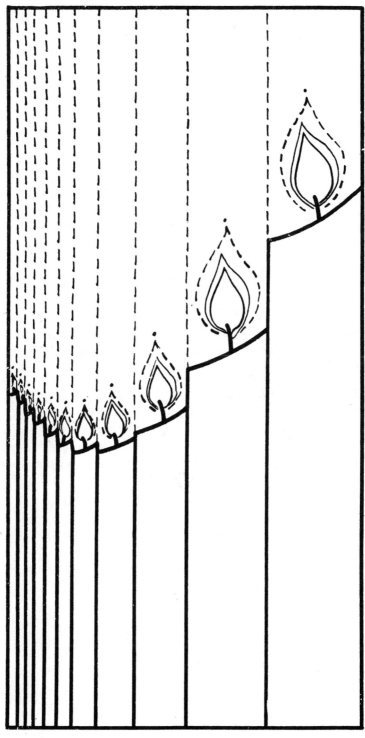

Light of the Spirit

The Holy Spirit is difficult to depict graphically since it is invisible, and is represented by various symbols in the Bible. But what the Spirit looks like is less important than what it does.

The third design symbolizes the personal effect of the Holy Spirit has as it enters the heart of an individual believer. The cross-shaped hole shows that Christ has already prepared the way. The combination of heart (God's love), cross (Christ's resurrection), and dove (the Spirit's nurturing) also makes this design symbolic of the Holy Trinity.

Use straightforward colors for this banner: a dark color for the background, bright red for the heart, and white for the dove. The three shapes in this design are very strong, and they can tell the story alone. The banner would be effective done simply in cut paper or felt. Using different textured fabrics adds a little richness: a slightly rough homespun for the background, a shiny fabric for the heart, and a slightly napped fabric like velour for the dove.

Indwelling of the Spirit

The last design illustrates the Pentecost event described in Acts 2. Each person is touched with a tongue of fire and begins to speak in a different language. I made another version of this banner several years ago. I had stylized people shapes at the bottom of the banner. They looked something like fat bowling pins. I realized that I did not need to represent a whole human body. Showing just the heads was enough to capture the excitement and to suggest that the people were speaking. But the problem was to simplify the facial features as much as possible, and still show the emotion and action. Tilting the heads and placing them unevenly helped express the feeling. A straight row of heads, evenly spaced, would not suggest the same thing.

The people are at the very bottom of a long narrow banner. The background is pieced from vertical strips of fabric. Both of these compositional devices help suggest that the Spirit is descending from far above. If you have a place for an extra long banner, 15 to 20 feet, this design can be extended to that length.

Choose four or five middle value bright colors in the orange-red-purple range for the strips and the facial features of the people. Use a set of colors in the same range, but of very dark values, for the heads of the people. For example, an orange strip would end with a rust brown head, a red-orange strip would end with dark brown, and a red strip would end with maroon. The flames are made of bright yellow felt, with torn, fuzzy edges.

As you plan and work on banners for Pentecost, may the grace of the Lord Jesus Christ, the love of God, and the fellowship of the Holy Spirit be with you all.

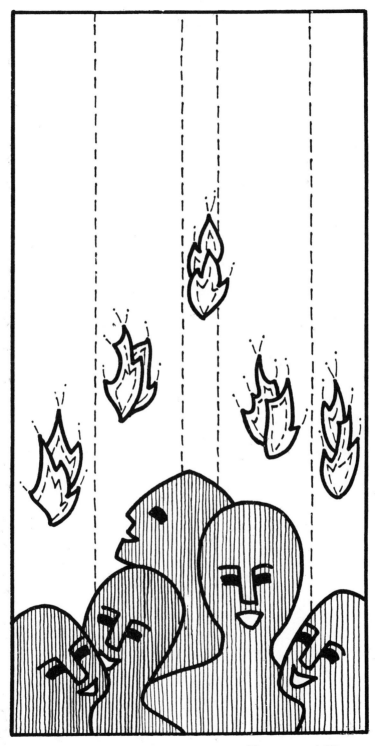

Tongues of Flame

7. TRINITY

FATHER, SON AND HOLY SPIRIT

The traditional symbol of the Trinity, three inter-connected rings, expresses the idea of Three-In-One, One-In-Three very well. In trying to come up with an alternate design to suggest the Trinity, I concentrated on the activity of each of the three persons in the God-head. God is love, so I started with a heart. God loved the world so much he sent his only son to die for us. The cross as the instrument of Christ's death is by far the most used Christian symbol. But Christ not only died, he also arose from the dead, so the cross shape in the design is hollow or empty to symbolize both the death and the empty tomb. Finally the spirit appeared at Pentecost in the form of tongues of fire, a source of energy and light, a life-giving force. This is a variation of the Pentecost design in the previous chapter.

This banner is effective made in a conventional way with a red heart and yellow and orange flames against a white background. However, a simple design like this can be also worked out with more exciting materials and techniques. Since the whole feeling of Pentecost is one of movement and energy, try using glowing shades of red, pink, and orange that vibrate against each other. Reflective materials, like satin, add life to the design. Try padding or stuffing the heart and flames.

Father, Son and Holy Spirit

If making the flames is difficult, find photographs of fire
and look at other artists' interpretations of flames. I was
surprised to find that most flames are predominantly yellow, with only a little orange or red. I have used overlapping
layers of silk organdy for a flame-like effect. The cut edges
can be sealed with clear nail polish or left ragged. Torn felt
or layers of nylon net can also be used.

8. SPECIAL TOPICS

GOD'S POWER AND MAJESTY

God's power and majesty are shown in his creation. Many of the Psalms are songs of praise to God as he is revealed in nature. At the end of time, the Day of the Lord will come unexpectedly and dramatically. This banner expresses God's cosmic dimension. Color, texture and shape are used to suggest power and vastness. The lower left-hand part of the banner depicts darkness and turbulence, in contrast to the upper right-hand part which is full of light and peace.

The upper right-hand corner is made of white nylon organdy. The clouds are a thin, white cotton/polyester fabric; I happened to find a piece that had transparent stripes woven in. The horizontal stripes represent water and land, and are strips of blues and greens pieced together. The sun, moon and stars are made of gold and silver metallic fabric. All of these pieces are sewed to the back side of the organdy so that they are slightly obscured by the sheer white overlay. This creates a mystical, other-wordly effect.

For the rest of the banner I chose heavy, dark fabrics; corduroys, denims and velours in somber shades of grey, blue, purple and red. The irregular, diagonal strips that suggest craggy mountains are top-stitched, while the turbulent crests of the waves are zigzagged with white thread to suggest a bit of foam. The colors in this banner, especially in the left-hand part, do not need to be realistic. I used purplereds in the mountains to suggest fire, volcanoes and earthquakes.

Creation

God exhibited his power in another way when he rescued the Children of Israel from the exploitation of the Pharaoh and led them out of Egypt. Exodus 19 describes this deliverance in terms of an eagle who carries her young on her wings. The golden eagle in this design fills the entire width of the banner and her body separates the blue sky and clear yellow sun from the ugliness and death below. The bottom part of the banner represents the ten plagues that God inflicted on the Egyptians in order to force the release of the Children of Israel: blood, frogs, gnats, worms, dead animals, boils, hail, locusts, darkness and death. The challenge here was to find ugly fabrics for the bottom part of the banner, and make it as unpleasant as possible.

The Book of Revelation talks about the end of all things and in chapter 21, describes God's holy city of Jerusalem as a radiant and glowing place where there is no night, and where nothing unworthy passes through the gates. Visually this holy city looks mystical above a bank of clouds. This banner would be effective made in shades of white, tan, grey and light blue satin. The reflective quality of this fabric gives it a glow of its own. Outline the shapes with stitching in slightly darker colors, and try padding the shapes so the play of light and shadow is intensified.

God Saves the Children of Israel

Another technical approach to depicting an other-worldly scene is to use bright, medium value colors: turquoise, medium purple, bright pink and bright gold. Build the city from blocks of these colors, then cover the whole thing with sheer white organdy. The colors will show through, but in a veiled way. Outline the shapes of the buildings with white stitching. The clouds at the bottom are dark grey, not covered with the white organdy.

The circle in this design is not meant to enclose the subject. It is a device to emphasize what we are looking at, like a word that is circled in a magazine article. We are being shown a preview of heaven; the circle symbolizes that eternity is endless. Since this circle is not a confining element, it should be merely suggested with stitching.

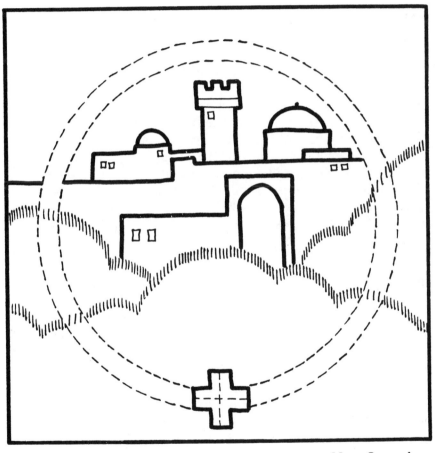

New Jerusalem

DEATH AND LIFE

As Christians, we feel deep grief in the presence of death. At the same time, however, we affirm life after death, and our despair is mixed with hope and joy. The Roman numerals I-X at the bottom of the first banner stand for the ten commandments: the laws God gave to show that we are sinners and doomed to death. The shapes of the Roman numerals are heavy and rigid. Rising up out of this dense mass is an empty cross symbolizing Christ's resurrection. The arms of the cross are like paths leading up and out. The center of the cross is suffused with glowing light. God sent his Son to die for us, so that, imperfect as we are, we can still claim God's love and grace through eternity.

The design itself is appropriate for Holy Week, Easter, or a funeral. The occasion for which it is used may influence the color you choose for the background. Make the Roman numerals from black felt, and the arms of the cross from white felt. The overlapping circles of light are made from layers of white nylon tulle, chiffon or organdy. A dark grey background gives the banner a somber, formal feeling, while a bright yellow background makes the design joyful and exuberant. If you like to do embroidery or applique, you can enrich the circles of light with decorative stitching or radiating shapes. Consider using a bit of metallic silver or gold in this part of the banner, but keep the overall feeling light.

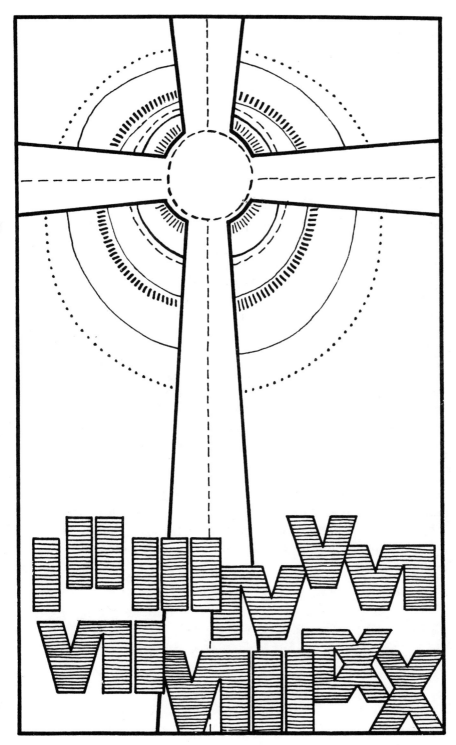

Law and Gospel

The second design is based on the text, John 14:1-14, "In my Father's house there are many rooms." The design can be used for a funeral or an occasion on which you wish to emphasize the assurance of life after death.

The clouds at the bottom indicate a heavenly location. While the New Jerusalem in the previous chapter is presented as a somewhat remote promise for the future, the house of many rooms is closer to us, and the lighted path leads us to the open door.

Since a house looks particularly inviting at night with light glowing through all the windows, imagine this banner with a dark blue or black building, silhouetted against a dark grey sky. The door and windows are glowing rectangles of bright yellow. I once made another version of this banner in which the windows were all the same size, arranged in even rows. The building looked cold and institutional. Windows varied in shape and placement make the house look much more appealing. Make the clouds of thin white fabric, letting a hint of the shapes underneath show through. The bright yellow path cuts through the clouds, clearly showing us the way to God's heavenly home.

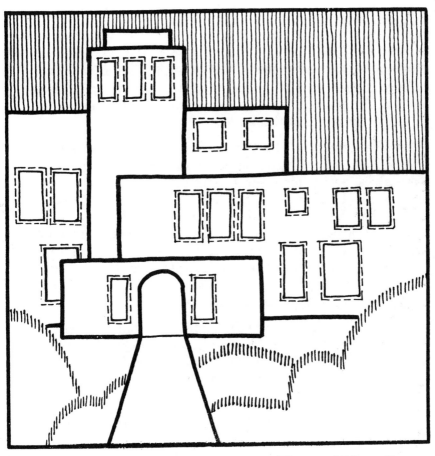

House of Many Rooms

HUNGER

We thank God for all gifts, but especially for a bountiful supply of food. Having enough to eat is something most of us take for granted. This banner reminds us that hunger is a specter in much of the world.

The arrangement of fruits and vegetables on the left is colorful and appealing. I chose these particular fruits and vegetables partly for their interesting shapes and colors, and partly because they appear often in our diet. Depict foods that are specific to your geographical area: citrus fruits and avocados in Southern California, wheat and corn in the mid-west, and orchard fruits in the Great Lakes area. The fruits and vegetables are made with a variety of fabrics in rich colors and textures. The shapes are rounded and padded to suggest health and vitality.

The starving child on the other side of the banner presents a stark contrast. The figure is flat and grey against a color-less background. There is no padding. The black outline, machine zigzagged, is angular and concave, suggesting withering and death.

The circular shape in this banner encloses both the bounti-ful harvest and the starving child. It forces us to recognize that both conditions exist in our world. This banner asks if it is God's will that we enjoy a disproportionate share of his bounty, while others, who are also his children, suffer from want.

Hunger

BREAD

Bread is mentioned many times in the Old Testament and in the Gospels. On some occasions it is a basic everyday food. At other times it takes on a supernatural aspect: God sent bread to the Children of Israel in the desert, and when Christ instituted the Eucharist, he equated bread with his own body. Let us see how one topic, "Bread," can be developed into several different designs.

Many of us have known the story of the Loaves and Fishes since we were children. To really appreciate the miracle that took place, we must look at the story from an adult perspective; that of a host or hostess planning a dinner. Imagine preparing enough food for eight or ten people, then having thousands arrive. Like the disciples, we'd say, "No way!" and probably not even attempt to feed anyone. The scale of the elements in the first banner emphasizes the discrepancy between the huge number of people and the two small fish and the five little loaves. Depicting this impossible situation verifies, as a true miracle, the fact that Jesus *was* able to feed everyone.

The people are massed together, and there is only enough detail to merely suggest individuals. The whole shape can be cut out as one piece. If you use felt, holes in the shape of faces can be cut out, and the piece can be laid over a brown fabric which shows through the holes to form the faces. The area is slightly padded so that the stitched or quilted lines produce a texture that defines the interior shapes. I suggest white robed people with brown faces on a sand

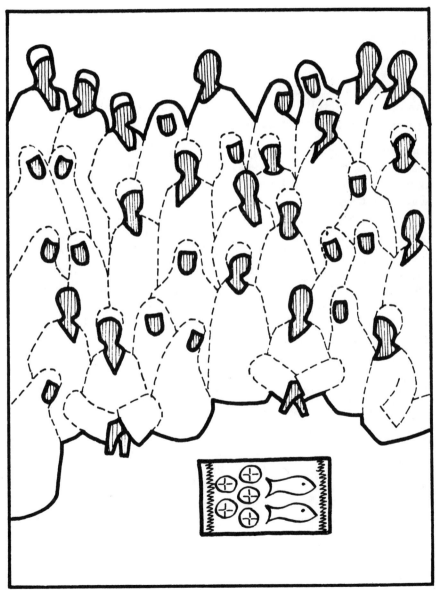

Loaves and Fishes

colored background. By contrast, the five loaves and two fish are distinct pieces, laid out carefully and separately on a white napkin. Each piece of food is made as a separate, stuffed shape, like doll house food. Then, it is attached to the banner. Metallic silver fabric covered with a sheer layer of dark purple, grey or brown, makes nice-looking fish.

Instead of illustrating a story, the second banner generalizes the idea that all our food is a gift from God. This design is appropriate for the harvest season; it depicts the sun and water that produce the wheat, which, in turn, is the source of bread, the staff of life. The shapes are stylized and interrelated, and arranged in a geometric way. Use clear, bright colors: sky-blue background, golden-yellow sun, burnt-orange wheat, and blue-green water. Zigzag the outline of the kernels and the beards, perhaps with dark yellow thread. The stems can be made with a double row of zigzagging. If you have trouble with the zigzag stitch tunneling or puckering, stabilize the back of the fabric with iron-on interfacing, or lay a piece of crisp, medium weight paper, like typing paper, on the back side. Sew through both the fabric and the paper, then tear away the excess paper. It is sometimes hard to get rid of every bit of paper, so plan to line the banner if you use this method.

If you don't want to tackle a big banner, this design makes a nice mini-banner. Applique the sun circle and the wheat. The water can be either appliqued or embroidered. Detailed handwork is a beautiful way to enrich a small banner that will be seen from close up.

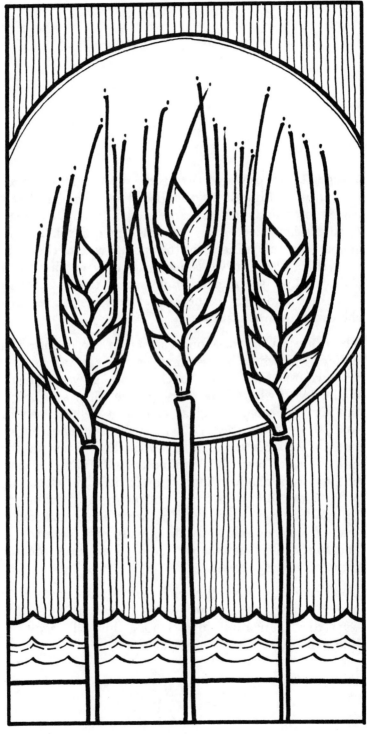

God Gives Bread

Jesus not only provided the people with ordinary bread, but he spoke of himself as the Bread of Life. This spiritual aspect of bread has its expression in the Eucharist. The third design focuses on the sacramental elements. The shapes are magnified to the point where they exclude everything else and we concentrate only on the bread and the wine. We are almost immersed in them. Compare the scale of this design to the Loaves and Fishes, which views the event from a distance.

There are several possibilities for the use of fabric in this design. The whole banner may be made of felt and bonded or sewn together: black background, grey outline of the chalice with white reflections, purple wine, and brown and tan for the bread. A glass chalice is represented in this case, so the light grey of the glass forms only a narrow outline, indicated in the drawing by the heavy line and the thin line. Areas of black background show through. As an alternative, try a chalice made of metallic silver cloth cut as a solid piece. Follow the heavy outline in the drawing and disregard the interior details. The bread looks textured if it is made from a double knit fabric, or from a cloth that is soft and fuzzy. This banner can be used anytime you want to focus on the Eucharist.

God's Word is incredibly rich, and there are many levels and meanings to explore. We've looked at three different ways to visualize one idea. I hope this will inspire you to find even more.

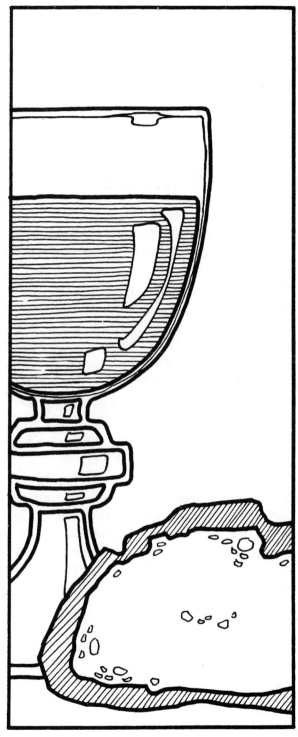

Christ's Body and Blood

SALT AND MUSTARD

God gives us bread, the basic staff of life. In turn our faith is equated to salt and mustard seed, small but potent and meant to be used.

The salt shaker is shown spilling the salt crystals so that they can give out their flavor and preservative properties. I used a dark blue background and a white and grey salt shaker with a metallic silver lid. It was more of a problem than I had anticipated to find an example of the quintessential faceted glass salt shaker to work from.

The salt crystals are small rectangles of iron-on interfacing, fused to the banner. I stitched a few vertical lines through the padded background to give some additional texture and body, and to emphasize the vertical path of the salt crystals.

The mustard seed emphasizes the contrast between a tiny beginning and a tremendous result. A few little mustard seeds near the bottom of the banner are surrounded by empty space to make the seeds seem even smaller. The thriving mustard plant at the top is so big, we can see only the bottom of it. We have to imagine how big the whole plant must be. In a sense, the plant is boundless; it cannot be contained within the banner.

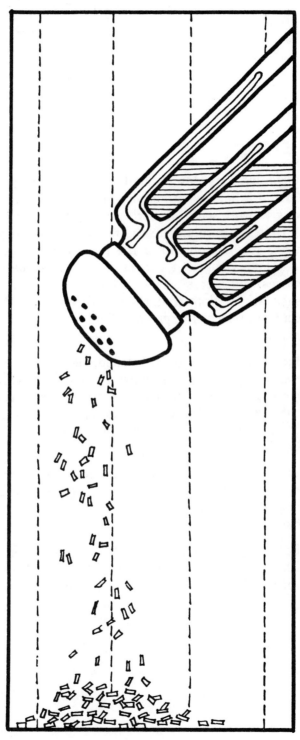

Stay Salty

Visualize this design made with leaf-green or olive-green felt on a light, summer-sky-blue background. A convenient way to work with an intricate shape like this is to draw the outline of the plant on the felt with a sliver of soap. Then, place the felt on top of the blue background, and pin the two layers together. Stitch just inside the outline of the leaves and stems as you attach the two layers of cloth to each other. Note that the empty space at the bottom is a continuation of the green felt; it is all in one piece with the plant.

When the stitching is finished, begin to cut away the unwanted areas of felt to allow the blue background to appear between the leaf shapes. The advantage of sewing first and cutting last is that you will not have to struggle to keep a lot of little pieces in position. This method is not a lot faster, but it gives a neater result.

Bright yellow felt flowers and the seeds are sewn on last, perhaps with French knots. Incidentally, *cruciferae* is the botanical name for the mustard plant because the flower has four petals in the shape of a cross.

Both of these banners are examples of designs that have a Christian meaning only to people who are already familiar with the Bible passages upon which they are based.

Mustard Seed

PROTECTION

As our heavenly father, God offers us mercy, protection and comfort. Examples are given of his compassion for birds and animals to show that if he cares for these creatures, how much more he must care for us who are his children.

To illustrate God's concern for the birds, picture a sparrow, a common bird of no commercial value. Make it very life-like, with brown, black and white felt and machine or hand embroidery. Look at a picture in a bird watcher's handbook to get the correct markings. In contrast to the small, realistic bird, the large, stylized hands of God are subtly suggested by lines of quilting on the rust-orange background.

I framed this particular banner with a broad strip of printed fabric at the top and bottom to produce a hanging for my home. Any kind of border will enhance the idea of a protective God.

In the sparrow design, scale is an important element. The sparrow is small in relation to the hands, and it is located near the bottom of the banner to show how unimportant and vulnerable it is. The large, compassionate hands of God come down from the top and fill more than half the space. There is no indication of depth in the design. We feel a sense of intimacy with what is happening because the bird and the hands both seem close to us.

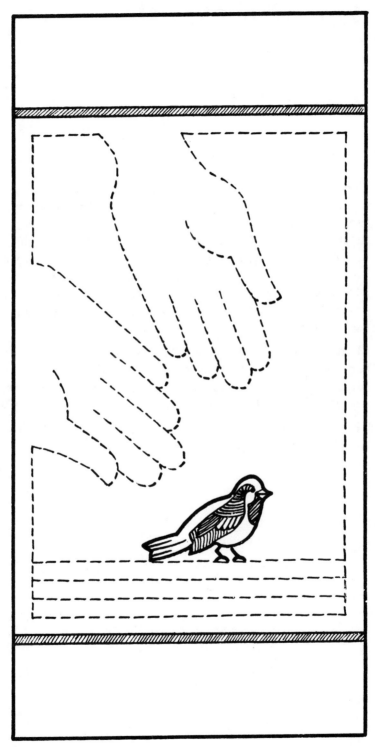

God Cares for the Sparrows

The image of the Lord as a shepherd is a much used illustration of his protection and care. Texture is an important part of this design. Choose fabrics that are soft and fuzzy, and pad the banner with quilt batting so that the shapes are rounded and yielding. Try a medium to dark blue velour for the sky and green velour for the grass. The shepherd's robe can be made from striped velour or corduroy and, of course, the sheep are constructed from synthetic fleece.

Make the face and hands of the shepherd and the faces, ears, and hoofs of the sheep from felt. Embroider the features by hand or machine, or draw them on with a waterproof pen. Then glue or bond the felt shapes in place.

This banner is particularly appealing to children because of the soft textures, and it makes up well as a mini-banner.

Good Shepherd

HEALING

Healing was an important part of Jesus' ministry. He cleansed lepers, gave sight to the blind and hearing to the deaf, restored the crippled and paralyzed, cast out the demons of those who were in emotional and spiritual anguish, and cured many diseases. Instead of concentrating on specific infirmities, here are some designs that generalize the idea of physical and spiritual healing.

Two healing, peace-giving hands reach down to those that are groping, crippled, weak, anguished and angry. "Reach out and touch somebody."

Keep the background dark; try black, wine red, or dark blue. The healing hands are white. Make the suffering hands from various colors; try bright, clashing, non-human colors like purple, orange, and blue-green, or a variety of printed fabrics. Most all fabrics will work. This design could also be painted, or made from cut paper. Attach the hands to the background with machine stitching, zigzagging iron-on bonding web, glue; whatever works with the material you choose.

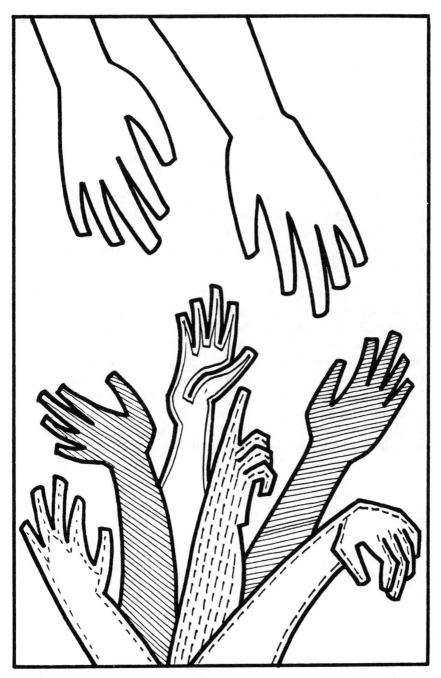

Healing Hands

A plump, bright heart, filled with the Holy Spirit is contrasted to dull, mis-shapen, sin-filled hearts, and those who are broken hearted, hard hearted, heavy hearted, and heart sick.

Again, the background is dark; I used black. The spirit-filled heart is bright red, the dove is white, and the sin-filled hearts are dark; dull reds, purples and browns. Use fabric in a variety of textures and weights. The dove is effective in a satiny fabric.

Make each heart like a little pillow by stitching front and back together, then turning the piece right side out. Construct the two wings and the body of the dove in the same way. Stuff the spirit-filled heart and the dove so they look plump and firm. Leave some of the sin-filled hearts unstuffed and shriveled; stuff others unevenly. The sin-filled hearts are irregular in shape and size and may be slightly torn, have threads hanging out, and show other imperfections. After the individual hearts and parts of the dove are completed, hand stitch them to the background.

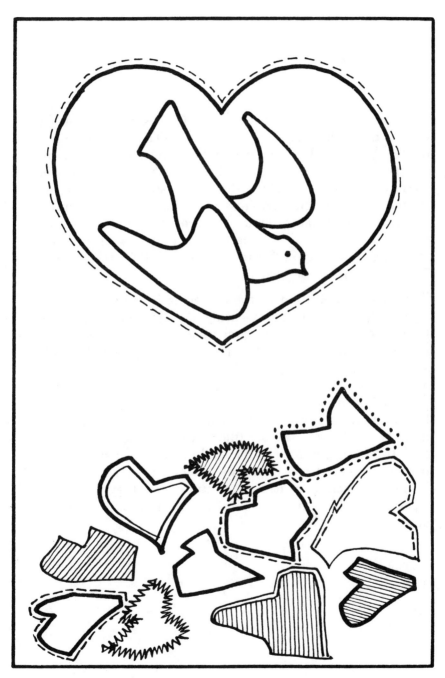

Sin-filled Hearts

The doll banner expresses the idea of being made whole in Christ, both physically and spiritually. The broken doll is tossed into a dark corner while the whole, upright figure stands solidly in the center of the cross shape. The cross is made of a lighter, brighter shade of color than the background. For example, the cross could be bright red against a dark wine-red background. The broken figure is black or grey to contrast to the whole figure in white with a living red heart. A variety of fabrics will also work for this design. Try red satin for the heart.

The basic composition of these designs is the same; a big element at the top, representing the desired state, contrasted to several smaller elements at the bottom that represent the undesirable. While the hands and the dolls work as well as graphic design as they do in fabric, the effectiveness of the heart banner depends on the characteristics of cloth wrinkled, raveled, stuffed, etc. The colors used in the bottom part of each design should look unpleasant, even ugly. When I made the sin-filled hearts, I used scraps left over from various articles of clothing I had made in the past. Of course, I had originally chosen the fabrics because I thought each was attractive. But when they were put together, I came up with a definitely unwholesome combination.

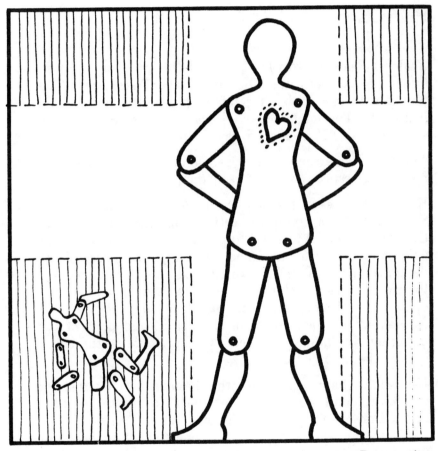

Re-creation

PEACE

Shalom! Peace be to you! Forms of this greeting are used frequently in both the Old and New Testaments. The phrase expresses wishes for safety, prosperity, health, and happiness. The modern day equivalent might be, "Have a safe trip!" or "Have a good day!"

The first banner depicts two people embracing. They have not let differences come between them. They are united.

Keep the figures in the banner simple, almost cartoon-like. Since we are not trying to portray romantic love, simplify the hair and facial features to the point where they suggest neither male nor female. The most important part of the design is posture and gesture. The figures are pressed together, faces touching, arms intertwined, and hands open. The figures seem to be close to the viewer. I eliminated the lower parts of the bodies and most of the background. These didn't seem to contribute to the closeness of the embrace.

Use bright, happy colors for this banner. I chose rust for the background, yellow-gold for the figure in the middle, and red-orange for the figure at the left. In the past, I have tried making similar figures all in one color, but the result was dull and flat. This time I pieced the garments together from two or three slightly different shades of the same color and added stripes of contrasting colors. I used scraps of cloth that had accumulated from other projects. The result was a rich and cheerful surface.

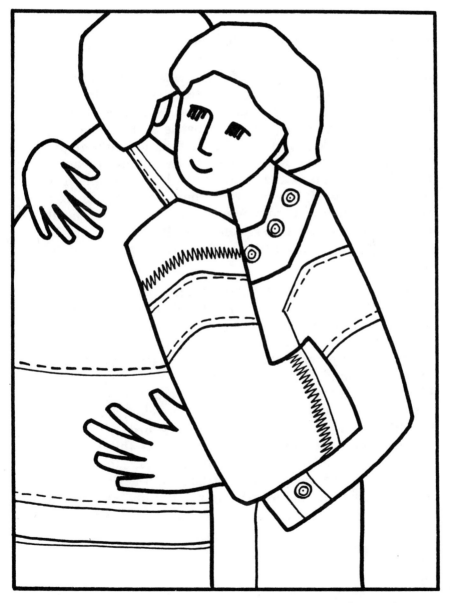

Reconciliation

To many people, peace is the absence of war, an anti-military state. The second chapter of Isaiah speaks about this, especially verse four: "He will settle disputes among great nations. They will hammer their swords into plows and their spears into pruning knives. Nations will never again go to war, never prepare for battle again." The King James translation describes the first agricultural implement in this verse as a plowshare. It was not until I realized that the plowshare is the blade at the bottom of the plow that I understood how a sword could so easily be converted. Although modern plows are made entirely of metal, plows from biblical times were probably wooden implements with only the cutting blade at the bottom made of metal.

Make the sword blade and the plowshare both of metallic silver cloth to emphasize how much alike they are. The top part of the plow can also be silver, or it can be brown like the shaft and the handle. To emphasize the sinister and destructive property of the sword, place it on a dark purple-blue background. A narrow dark red stripe, suggestive of blood, extends from the point of the sword. By contrast, on the other side, the plow is working through strips of dark brown earth and bright green grass, against a turquoise summer sky. The point of the plow gives this design a definite direction. As it is pictured here, it is moving from right to left, and would work best hung on the right side of a room, pointing toward the front. Simply reverse the design if you want it to move in the opposite direction.

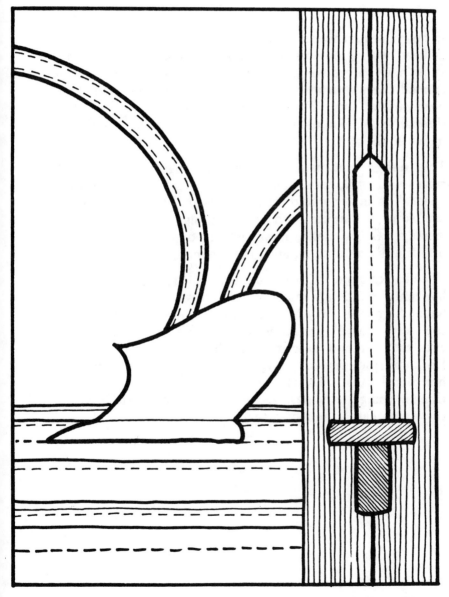

Swords into Plows

In both our earthly and spiritual lives, we are sometimes so deluged with problems, demands, and fears that we don't know how we are going to survive. Mark 4 tells how Jesus calmed the storm and the disciples when it seemed their boat would sink. This banner design reminds us that through faith, God assures us we can find peace even in the midst of the storm.

This design contrasts the grasping, engulfing shapes of waves with still, calm, horizontal bands of color. The word "peace" is incorporated into the design. Ordinarily I don't use words in banners and let the design alone convey the message. Occasionally, however, one or two words can fit into the design and enhance the meaning.

The background of this banner is grey. The central, horizontal bands are made of light, bright blue-greens, perhaps of smooth, silky fabrics. The top horizontal band and the word "peace" are made of white felt in the "sew first, cut last" method described in the chapter on applique. Dark purple-grey or purple-blue waves surround the horizontal area. Sew the edges of the waves with white thread, using the widest zigzag stitch. The fabric used for the waves can be rough in texture, like denim.

Peace, Be Still

The ultimate kind of peace, complete trust in God, is expressed in Psalm 4: "When I lie down, I go to sleep in peace; you alone, O Lord, keep me perfectly safe." The sleeping figure in this design is small and vulnerable. But the person is completely protected by the gentle hand of God.

Sandwich quilt batting or synthetic fleece between the front and lining of this banner, then simply outline the shape of the hand with stitching. This quilted outline will show up best if the background is a fairly light color: off-white, tan or gold. Make the sleeping figure in a darker color, and use the same shade to bind the edges of the banner. The binding, along with bands of the same fabric at the top and bottom, create a border or frame that enhances the feeling of security and protection. Add stars or decorative quilting to the rest of the background if you think it looks too empty. A monochromatic color scheme works well for this design; tan or yellow-gold sky with a brown figure and border and metallic gold stars in the sky. Or a light blue sky, dark blue figure and border, with silver stars. Find a combination that is appealing and restful.

Sleep in Peace

LOVE

When I look back over the banners I've designed, I realize that several of them include a heart. Although some people associate hearts with a sentimental, Valentine kind of love, to me the heart expresses the center of my Christian faith — God's love for me and all His creation.

Two figures, the larger one with its arm around the smaller, seem to symbolize God's relationship with his children. This relationship includes the ideas of protection and salvation. I added a single heart to show that this is a union created through love. The larger figure completely surrounds the smaller, with one arm embracing it and with the other arm showing or teaching it.

Ordinarily I'd emphasize that the larger figure is the superior protector by making it darker. But in this case, we can inject a visual paradox to suggest the mystery of the relationship, by making the larger figure lighter and the smaller figure darker. In this way, the smaller figure has a more definite physical reality while the larger figure is not so easy to perceive and seems more spiritual.

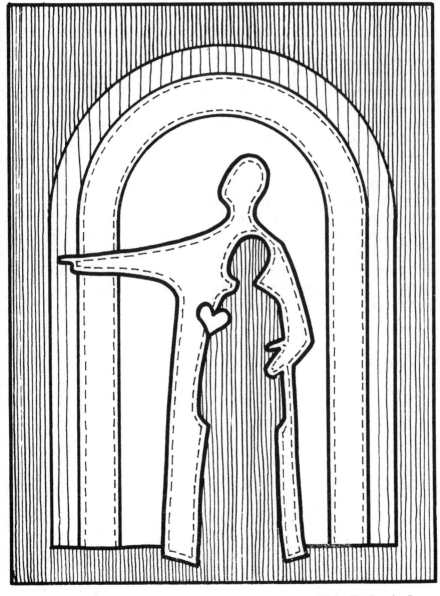

The Father's Love

The figures are enclosed in an arch shape, another device to suggest protection and shelter. The outer arch is dark like the smaller figure, to tie these two elements together and place them nearest the viewer in the physical world. The arches grow lighter as they converge toward the larger figure in the center of the banner. This effect draws the viewer through a dark doorway into a glorified world of light.

The colors themselves, except possibly for the bright red heart, are not as important as the light and dark relationships. Start with a dark blue, brown, grey or green and create a progression from there to white or yellow. Or, in a different approach, use an assortment of bright colors, at the same time still being careful to go from dark to light. Enhance the progression with texture; go from rough to smooth, from thick to thin, or from opaque to sheer.

Love Each Other

The love God offers energizes my life and helps me, in turn, to give love back to God in the form of obedience, and give it out to other people in the form of service.

This is the relationship expressed in the hearts and hands design. It was made originally for Stewardship Sunday, but has become a favorite and is used often. It was fun to sew, using patchwork techniques with many shades and textures of red and brown fabric. Because the pieces are small, I mostly used scraps. Technically, the piecing is not perfect, but the overall glow of color and the radiating design makes the banner come alive.

Christian obedience is inspired by love. In Mark 8, we are admonished to take up our cross and follow Christ. We respond actively and willingly to this command. In this banner the crosses are lifted up with love. Make the background and the figures at the bottom from a dark color so that the white-robed Christ figure predominates, both in scale and in color value. Make Christ's halo out of bright, glorious colors, so that they relate to the bright red hearts. Our love is part of His glory.

Lift Up Your Hearts

9. TECHNIQUES

FABRICATION

My primary concern in this book is the subject of banner design. In this chapter I would like to talk briefly about banner fabrication; some tricks and shortcuts I use when I put a banner together. These techniques reflect the fact that most of my banners are machine sewn, appliqued, and two dimensional. Let us assume that you have worked out a good design, have a small sketch, and are ready to make the banner.

The choice of fabric can make the difference between success and failure. The background fabric must be firm and stable; knitted fabrics and stretchy woven fabrics give nothing but trouble. Heavy cottons and cotton blends like denim, corduroy and sailcloth are easy to work with. Lighter fabrics, and even sheer fabrics will take more careful handling, but will work as long as they don't have much stretch. If you must keep costs down, search remnant tables, and keep an eye open for sheets and bedspreads at white sales and rummage sales. Newark Dressmaker Supply, Box 2448, Lehigh Valley, PA 18001, a mail-order firm, sells 81″ wide cotton/polyester sheeting at very reasonable price.

Felt, that old banner stand-by, can't be beat for small, intricate pieces, because the edges don't need to be finished. But I like to use other fabrics for the background of the banner and for the bigger, simpler appliqued pieces. That way I have a much larger variety of colors and textures to work with. Felt comes in a frustratingly limited number of colors and I have succeeded in dying white felt with Rit dye to get subtle colors for small areas of a banner. Don't use extremely hot water when dying felt. Other than small pieces of felt and linings made from sheets, I don't often dye fabrics. Unless you are willing to learn a little about the chemistry of dying, it's hard to be sure you'll get the color you want, and that it will be light-fast.

Here are a couple of ways to enlarge your small sketch to a full size pattern for the banner. The grid system is the most familiar. If you want the finished banner to be 3'×5', divide the small sketch into three squares by five squares. Then transfer the design from each small square onto a paper pattern marked off into one foot squares. I make big pieces of paper for patterns by gluing cut-up brown paper grocery sacks together. Newspaper offices will often sell the ends of newsprint rolls for a reasonable price. If you have access to an overhead projector, you can enlarge your design with it. Make a line drawing with a permanent felt pen on a piece of transparent acetate. Or have a drawing on paper transferred to acetate at your local copy shop. Some people hang the cloth on the wall, project the design directly onto it, then mark or cut the shapes. By the way, a small sliver of dry soap makes a good marker.

If you plan to machine-sew the banner, there is a limit to the size you can maneuver under the machine. A piece bigger than a king-size bed is going to be difficult. I find that straight pins have the habit of popping out when I crunch a big piece under the presser foot of the machine. A large piece also tends to hang over the edge of the table and pull. It helps to secure the pieces together firmly before sewing by lots of basting, or with glue. I like Unique Stitch glue, which comes in a tube, and I also use iron-on bonding web, like Stitch Witchery. A big banner is easier to make if it is designed to be made in separate sections or units, which are put together at the last stage.

The technique of applique consists of cutting out small pieces and applying them to a background. With fabrics like felt, and some knits (which arc okay when applied as small pieces to a stable background), there is no need to finish the edges. The edges of fabrics which ravel are usually turned under or covered with a decorative stitch such as zigzagging. I have sealed the edges of sheer synthetic fabrics by searing them in a candle flame or painting them with clear lacquer. Fingernail polish works on small pieces.

Sometimes I line banners in order to hide messy stitching on the back side, or to give more stability to a piece so it will hang well. The easiest way to line a banner is to lay the lining piece on the banner, right sides together, and stitch all around the edge, leaving an opening big enough to turn the whole thing right-side-out. If the banner looks all right on the back side, and is sturdy, or if you want a sheer effect, you can hem or bind the edges. A binding can show like a frame on the front of the piece, or can be turned all the way to the back, whichever looks better in relation to the design of the banner.

My favorite way to hang a banner is with a piece of PVC: plastic plumbing pipe. PVC is inexpensive, lightweight, strong, and easy to cut. I insert a piece of PVC into a hem or casing at the top of the banner. I string a length of sash cord through the pipe and tie the ends together, then slide the knot to the inside of the pipe. This makes a sturdy, invisible, utilitarian hanging system. If the design of your banner or the occasion calls for a decorative rod, use a wooden dowel, aluminum pipe, lucite rod, or a fancy curtain rod. Just be sure the hanging system doesn't call attention away from the banner itself.

The practical things to think about when making a banner are its size, its weight, how it will be used (for example, if it will be carried or stationary), where it will hang, and how it will hang. Do whatever works, and you will find yourself inventing new techniques as you go along.

APPLIQUE

Most of my banners are shapes cut out of fabric and applied to a background. Here are some applique techniques I use for fabric. Some can be used with paper as well.

Fastening the Shape to the Background

Sewing — Hand stitching can be invisible. Both hand and machine stitching range from a simple running stitch to elaborate embroidery. Zigzagging and decorative stitching may provide strength, hide a raw edge, add an accent, enrich texture, or add small details.

Gluing and bonding — White glue works for materials that are not too thin. I like Unique Stitch, a fabric glue that comes in a tube. Bonding web, such as Stitch Witchery, is cut and sandwiched between the shape and the background. When ironed, it fuses the two pieces together. It is especially good for large pieces.

How to Treat the Edges of the Shapes

Edges turned under — This is the traditional method of applique. For a smooth edge, machine stitch slightly outside the fold line and clip the curves. Then fold under the edge, just inside the machine stitching. Stitch the shape to the background, just inside the fold.

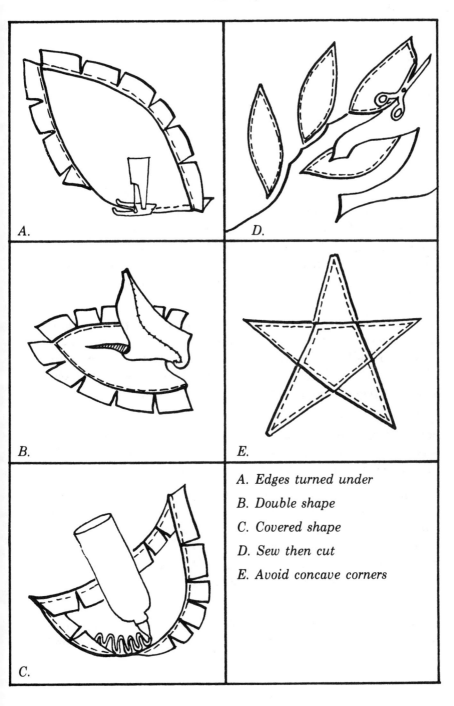

A. *Edges turned under*

B. *Double shape*

C. *Covered shape*

D. *Sew then cut*

E. *Avoid concave corners*

A covered shape — Cut an inner shape of a stiff material like felt, heavy interfacing or light cardboard; then cover it with material, using the technique described just above. Wrap the edges of the material around the stiff shape, and glue them down on the back side. Stitch or glue the whole thing to the background. This method gives the shapes a padded look.

A double shape — Sew through two layers of fabric, right sides together, all the way around the edge of the shape. Make a small slit in the middle of the back side through which to turn the piece right-side-out. The slit will not show after the piece is attached to the background.

Unfinished edges — Non-woven materials like felt, nylon net, Pellon, paper and knits that do not ravel can be left the way they are. Woven fabric with a raveled edge can be left unfinished if the uneven edge contributes to the design.

Stabilized edges — Stabilize woven fabrics by bonding them to non-woven material and cut out the shapes after the two layers have been fused. Or paint the edges of woven fabrics with glue, clear nail polish, lacquer, acrylic paint, etc. Sometimes it is easier to paint first, and cut later when the paint is dry. Sear the edges of synthetic fabric in a candle flame.

Covered edges — Cover unfinished edges with zigzagging or other decorative stitching. Apply binding tape, ribbon, yarn, etc. by stitching or with glue.

For Easier Applique...

Plan the shapes to avoid complicated concave corners. Overlap pieces so hidden edges do not need to be finished. Combine patchwork and applique. If you are appliqueing many small pieces of the same material close to each other, draw them in their correct positions on a larger piece of material. If you are handsewing turned-under edges, cut an inch or two at a time along the cutting line, then fold under and stitch. If you are machine stitching raw edges, sew along all the outlines, then carefully cut away the top layer of material in between the shapes.

Ideas to Try

Apply shapes underneath a sheer "background." Cut two of each shape from non-woven material like felt or paper, then glue or stitch them together with a nylon net background sandwiched in between. Use subtle variations of the same color; both the right and wrong sides of the material; napped fabrics with the nap running in different directions.

BIG BANNERS: FABRICATION

Making big banners presents special problems. It seems like an overwhelming job to make an impact in a large sanctuary, and the cost of materials, the amount of time needed to make a big banner, and the process of putting it together are all magnified in proportion to the size of the finished piece. Since my experience with making very big banners has been limited, I asked readers of *Modern Liturgy* to share their expertise.

The first step in the construction of a banner, big or little, is making a small sketch of the design. Cheryl Hicks, of Albuquerque, New Mexico, sometimes enlarges her small drawings by the grid method. She tapes the background fabric to the floor, and marks a big grid on it by snapping a chalked line (a technique borrowed from carpenters). She also hangs the bare fabrics on the wall and projects her design onto it with an overhead projector.

The choice of fabric is important. Several readers warned against anything stretchy or loosely woven. Felt, which comes in six foot widths, is a favorite for big banners. Helene McGrath, Cincinnati, Ohio, doubles the felt for banners that are 12'×16'. Cheryl Hicks has used muslin for banners 16'×20', and canvas for banners as big as 20'×42'. Patty Linardos, Canoga Pak, California, likes to use the types of fabrics that are intended for upholstery and drapery, like cotton duck and antique satin; they are wide, and if the entire width is used, there is no need to hem the side edges.

An opposite approach is to use very lightweight fabrics. Nancy Chinn, San Anselmo, California, has made a series of angel banners, painted with acrylics on a sheer synthetic fabric. I have used nylon net, which has the advantage of being inexpensive and six feet wide, as the backing for shapes of felt or lightweight woven fabric (which is hand-basted onto the net). I have finished the edges of the shapes either by turning them under, in the traditional applique method, or by painting the outlines of each shape with clear lacquer, then cutting the shapes out after the lacquer is dry. The lacquered edge prevents raveling. I have also glued felt or paper shapes onto the net backing by cutting two copies of each shape, and gluing them together with the netting sandwiched between. These transparent banners are especially effective when they are hung in mid-air, and they have the added advantage of being lightweight.

Patti Vehec, Erie, Pennsylvania, and Patty Linardos both use non-raveling fabric, such as felt, double-knits, or bonded upholstery fabrics, from which to cut the shapes that form designs on the banners. The edges of the shapes need no further finishing, and they are pinned to the background with long quilting pins, then secured with large basting stitches. Patti Vehec first pins the shapes in place while the whole banner is spread out on the floor. Then she puts the banner into a quilting frame for basting. Many of her banners are 15'-18' long, and as wide as the fabric she has chosen. She uses the center fold of the background fabric as a guideline for placing the shapes, then steam presses the banner before hanging it. After the banners have been used, both women may later remove the basted-on shapes and re-use the background fabric for a different design. This cuts down considerably on the cost.

Patty Linardos estimates that a pair of banners, each 5'×16', takes 2-8 people, 1-5 days to sew, and the material costs $40-160. Each pair of banners hangs for one season in the liturgical year.

Cheryl Hicks feels that 12'×16' is about the largest size one person can manipulate through a sewing machine. She used a home sewing machine for one banner that was 16'×20', but she needed a second person to maneuver the fabric. She paints banners which are larger than this with water based latex paint or tempera mixed from a powder, and has not had any trouble with cracking, peeling, or fading.

Once you have succeeded in making a large banner, there is still the problem of hanging it. A couple of readers suggested sewing a hem, at least 4" wide, at the top and bottom of the banner. Insert a length of 1"×2" or 2"×4" lumber like a curtain rod. Cut slits in the top of the banner, several inches in from either end, to allow screw eyes to be fastened into the lumber. Suspend the banner with cords or ropes threaded through the screw eyes. I often use sash cord, available from the hardware store, to hang banners. It is strong and smooth without being too thick. If you are going to be hanging banners in the same place often, it is worthwhile to install permanent screw eyes or pulleys, so that the banners can easily be hoisted up and down.

For wrinkle-free transport and storage, roll the banners, design side out, around the heavy cardboard tubes that upholstery fabric comes on.

BIG BANNERS: DESIGN

Here are some design ideas that work well for big banners. I am talking about banners that are temporary (they hang for a few Sundays or a season) rather than works of art that are permanent parts of the church decor.

Color alone makes a big impact in a large space. Readers Helene McGrath of Cincinnati, Ohio, and Nancy Chinn of San Anselmo, California, both use colored panels to create a mood. Helene hangs three or four fabric panels on either side of the altar. She uses purple during Lent, then changes to bright rainbow colors for Easter. The colors in the Easter banners coordinate with banks of multi-colored flowering plants placed in front of the altar. Nancy hangs many fabric panels perpendicular to the wall along the sides of the sanctuary. These are arranged in color sequences depending on the mood she wishes to create. This idea has a lot of possibilities. Think of somber purples and blues for Lent, going from pale colors at the back of the church to deep colors at the front. Try a progression of bright red to yellow for Pentecost, mixed bright colors for Easter, and rose to blue for Advent.

In addition to the impact of the color itself, the placement and quantity of the colored panels contribute to the effect. Helene McGrath uses fewer panels, sometimes hung on only one side of the altar, for less festive occasions. Nancy Chinn sometimes hangs her panels at the front of the church, along the sides, or even at the back if she wants to influence the mood of the people as they go out from the service. I have found that hanging a banner over the pews like a canopy creates an intimate feeling suitable for Christmas or Pentecost, while placing a banner up high at the front of the church is more remote and majestic for the Resurrection and Ascension. Colored panels or banners at the entrance to the sanctuary, or even outdoors, create an inviting welcome and extend a friendly farewell.

Manipulating the cloth by draping, twisting, gathering, and folding is another technique that adds depth and helps create a mood. In Patti Vehec's church in Erie, Pennsylvania, they drape the Lenten cross. The drape is rigged with a rope and, during the Good Friday service, the rope is cut, the drapery falls to the floor, and the cross is revealed. On Easter, the cross, located on one side of the chancel, is draped in white. A white banner with a buttterfly stands on the other side of the chancel. This area is banked with ferns and palms and provides a setting for the baptism of new catechumens. In Peggy Linardos' church in Canoga Park, California, the Easter banner, emblazoned with "Alleluia, He is Risen," lies folded on the floor at the beginning of the Easter Vigil. It is hoisted into view during the singing of the "Gloria."

Work with the architecture of your sanctuary. I find the light ledges over the side aisles in my church provide a convenient place to attach lines from which to hang banners in mid-air. If you have a dome or apex, consider draping a line or length of fabric from it. During Lent, Nancy Chinn hangs a sheer drape from ceiling to floor on the wall behind the altar. The cloth partially obscures a round stained-glass window, and she exploits the round spot where the window shows through the cloth by framing it with a large crown of thorns. At Easter, the drape is removed to reveal the colors of the window in all their brilliance.

So far, I have not described many big banners that have designs, pictures, symbols, or words on them. I feel designs of the kind I usually make will not work as well at a super scale as they do at the more human scale of 3'×5' or 4'×6'. In addition to the question of the suitability of a design at a large scale, there is the problem of sewing or fabricating a complicated large design. One way to get around the fabrication problem is to work with smaller segments or modules, then combine them into a larger piece. Design the banners in strips, bands, or blocks which are constructed separately and then assembled. Quilt piecing and setting techniques can be adapted. For example, a medallion quilt has a central design surrounded by a border of strips. My mother, Wilda Carter of Fostoria, Ohio, has made a banner in which a cross shape is formed by four huge log cabin quilt blocks, set so the darker corners all meet in the center.

Several readers stressed the importance of keeping the design simple for large banners. Incorporate one symbol or one word on one panel of a series, and leave the rest of the panels plain. Simple symbols or designs can be attached to a panel for a few Sundays, then removed and replaced by different symbols for the following season. Peggy Linardos took the opposite approach. She sewed several words and symbols on the banner to start with, then covered them with pieces of cloth which formed a decorative pattern. The covers were removed Sunday by Sunday to reveal the words and symbols underneath.

Designing and making big banners is not easy. Keep in mind that they should work with the architecture of the sanctuary and the chancel furnishings. Instead of trying to design a work of art that will stand alone, design the banners to be a part of the whole liturgy. They create moods and amplify and enhance other things that are going on in the service. Although it is often necessary to have the help of other people when fabricating a big banner, it is usually one person who initiates the project and develops the completed design.

MINI-BANNERS

The word "banner" comes from an old Gothic root meaning "a sign." The dictionary defines a banner as a piece of cloth bearing an emblem or motto. We think of church banners as large fabric works, designed to be used in public worship.

But I also like to make small banners that express personal feelings. Recently I had fun working out a series of designs based on biblical passages about love. I decided that each banner should contain heart shapes, but that the hearts would be arranged differently so that each design expressed the idea of a specific bible text. Working on a small scale, (about the size of this page) allowed me to experiment with a variety of solutions to the design problem I had set for myself. As a bonus, I enjoyed digging through my scraps and making something beautiful from leftovers.

After looking at the many references under the word "love" in a concordance, I chose the following as having possibilities for interesting designs.

Love your neighbor as yourself (Matthew 22:39) suggested two equal hearts, partly merged together. I centered successively smaller double hearts, progressing from a dark red to bright red to shocking pink in the middle. Stitched on to a dark blue background, the hearts seemed to glow.

Love is eternal (1 Corinthians 13:8) seemed to call for a circular arrangement since a circle is an endless line. Once again, the hearts were equal in size and went through a color progression; rust, orange, yellow-orange, yellow,

Love Your Neighbor as Yourself

Love is Eternal

peach, orange, red, maroon. Unexpectedly, after I had appliqued the hearts to a dark brown background, I saw that the area in the center of the ring looked like a cross.

We love because God first loved us (1 John 4:19) reminds us that God's love was most strongly revealed in the death of Christ. Four hearts radiate from an equal-armed cross in this design. I also considered using one heart, quartered by the four arms of a superimposed cross.

Remain in my love (John 15:9) and **Nothing can separate us from the love of God** (Romans 8:38) can both be expressed by the contrast between a very large heart and a very small one attached to it or engulfed by it.

God loved the world so much that he gave his only son (John 3:16) is probably the best known verse in the bible. I think of this as a Christmas message and placed a red heart on a green background scattered with white stars.

I almost always make big banners on the sewing machine because it is faster. However, I enjoy stitching minibanners by hand. In fact, it seems easier to control the small shapes this way. Sometimes I like to stitch the words of the bible passage in the background or on the border with an inconspicuous thread. If you like to embroider, think of "God is love" (1 John 4:16) illustrated by a single big heart filled with outlines of flowers, insects, animals and people done with thread in a color similar to the heart so that from a distance, the pictures merge into the heart.

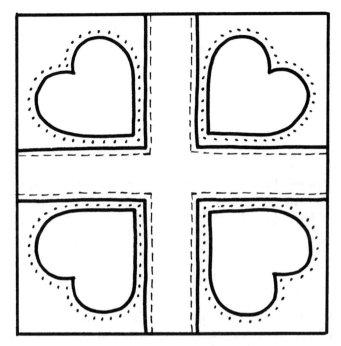

We Love Because God First Loved Us

We Love Because God First Loved Us

I've used hearts as a symbol of love to illustrate this chapter. But, of course, you can find an almost infinite number of ideas based on biblical texts; faith/fruits, enlightenment/light, growth/plants, the key objects in parables, modern-day objects as parables, service/hands, psalms in praise of the God of nature, etc. Color, texture and detail add richness to the arrangement of the shapes.

If you are hesitant about making a big banner for a public occasion, try making a mini-banner just for yourself. Be forewarned, however, that most of your mini-banners are probably destined to become very special gifts for the very special people in your life.

Remain in My Love

*God Loved the World So Much
(That He Gave His Only Son)*

10. APPENDIX

DESIGN CHECKLIST

THE IDEA

Select a theme, occasion or idea upon which to base a design.
Read, study, think, talk and pray about the theme.
Draw parallels, recall past experiences, compare related ideas.

★ PRIME THE PUMP!

then —

Distill, eliminate, generalize, enlarge, specialize, emphasize.
Throw away 95% of the ideas gathered in the first step.

★ FOCUS ON THE SINGLE STRONGEST IDEA

THE DESIGN

Manipulate design elements to support the idea.
COLOR – cool/warm, light/dark, bright/dull.
TEXTURE – ready-made or manipulated; folded
    gathered, wrinkled, padded.
FORM – shapes and lines express different feelings.
SYMBOL – pictures, words, icons. Be relevant. Beware
    of the out-of-date, the over-used. Be aware of
    cultural connotations.
COMPOSITION – relationship of forms and symbols to
    each other and to the space around them.
    Contrast: big/little, stable/active, sparse/dense,
    long view/close up.
    Progression, direction, movement, change.

Evaluate each design element. Does it support
the central idea? —— if not, eliminate it!

Experiment; evaluate what you are seeing.
Don't intellectualize too much.

★ TRUST YOUR FEELINGS!

| WHY I MAKE BANNERS |

Enhance, enrich, support worship in visual terms;
—— a temporary, changing element.
Communication, not decoration. Suggest ideas,
feelings, moods; recall stories, parables; ask
questions; pose paradoxes; express humor.

★ MY RESPONSE TO GOD'S WORD AND GOD'S GRACE!

Joe Knuth

BIBLICAL INDEX

TOPICAL INDEX

DESIGN AND FABRICATION INDEX

The pages listed after each topic may discuss that topic directly or be an illustration of that aspect of design or fabrication.